THE MAN FROM THE THIRD ROW

THE MAN FROM THE THIRD ROW

HASSE EKMAN, SWEDISH CINEMA AND THE LONG SHADOW OF INGMAR BERGMAN

Fredrik Gustafsson

berghahn
NEW YORK · OXFORD
www.berghahnbooks.com

Published in 2017 by
Berghahn Books
www.berghahnbooks.com
© 2017 Fredrik Gustafsson

Library of Congress Cataloging-in-Publication Data
Names: Gustafsson, Fredrik, 1974- author.
Title: The man from the third row : Hasse Ekman, Swedish cinema, and the long
shadow of Ingmar Bergman / Fredrik Gustafsson.
Description: New York : Berghahn Books, 2017. | Includes bibliographical
references and index.
Identifiers: LCCN 2016024919| ISBN 9781785332500 (hardback : alk. paper) |
ISBN 9781785332869 (pbk. : alk. paper) | ISBN 9781785332517 (ebook)
Subjects: LCSH: Ekman, Hasse--Criticism and interpretation. | Motion
pictures--Sweden--History.
Classification: LCC PN1998.3.E42 G87 2016 | DDC 791.4302/33092--dc23
LC record available at https://lccn.loc.gov/2016024919

British Library Cataloguing in Publication Data
A catalogue record for this book is available from the British Library

ISBN 978-1-78533-250-0 hardback
ISBN 978-1-78533-286-9 paperback
ISBN 978-1-78533-251-7 ebook

Contents

List of Illustrations

Acknowledgements

Many have helped me, inspired me and supported me in various ways when writing this book. I cannot name them all but among those that must be included are first of all Elisabetta Girelli at the University of St Andrews who has provided feedback on every single sentence. Second of all Helena Ekholm, who was an invaluable help regarding the images for the book, and Ola Törjas, both at the Swedish Film Institute. Then Marika Junström, the editor of *Filmrutan*, who has graciously let me publish articles about Hasse Ekman in that journal. Likewise I want to thank Mette Hjort and Ursula Lindqvist, the editors of Wiley-Blackwell's *A Companion to Nordic Cinema*, who asked me to contribute a chapter on Swedish cinema of the 1940s for their book. I also wish to thank the many scholars who have read and commented on the manuscript, including Arne Lunde, Brian Hoyle, Charles Drazin and Bjørn Sørenssen. Dave Kehr, presently at MoMA, deserves a special mention for helping me make Hasse Ekman better known in the world. And finally I thank Leif Furhammar, an excellent scholar and writer and an inspiring person, whose work has been so important to me. His sudden death as I had just finished writing the book was a shock, and it is with great sadness that I must accept that he will now never be able to read it.

Fortunately, life is not just film studies, and there are my dear friends and family members who have provided all sorts of help, inspiration and love. Among them I am particularly grateful to Amanda Eneroth and Lisa James Larsson, who have kept me sane and happy during these final years of writing.

As promised, the book is dedicated to Megan Dilly, who does better sand-surfing impressions than anyone I have ever met.

Introduction

'Have you failed as an artist?' asked the headline of a newspaper interview with the Swedish filmmaker and actor Hasse Ekman in 1967, two years after he had made his last film and moved from Sweden to Spain (Frankl 1967). It was a very unfair question, considering the rich body of work that Ekman had produced since the late 1930s, yet from another angle it was perhaps a valid question. Whereas most of his peers in the 1940s and 1950s, such as Ingmar Bergman and Alf Sjöberg, had become well known, even globally, and highly respected, Ekman had to some extent been forgotten in Sweden and never even discovered abroad. To use a famous expression, in Sweden Ekman had become an unknown known and outside Sweden (or at least outside Scandinavia) Ekman was, and remains, an unknown unknown. Why that should be is something of a mystery because Ekman was an important filmmaker and deserves the recognition he has never had. But it is never too late to be discovered, and it is hoped that this book will create an interest in Ekman, and even lead to retrospectives of his work at film festivals and cinematheques around the world. When he was at his best – roughly speaking, from 1945 to 1955 – he was an equal to any other filmmaker, and the films speak for themselves. But for them to be able to speak they must be seen, and for them to be seen there must be awareness of their existence.

This is not a biography but a scholarly study of Ekman's films, and since it is the first such study in English, all of his films will be discussed. For the sake of convenience his career will be assessed chronologically. This is relevant because Ekman's career followed a certain trajectory, whereas thematically the films are fairly consistent from beginning to end. But the book is not just about Ekman; it is also about the country in which he was born and in which he worked: Sweden. On the one hand, Ekman was an important figure in what can be said to be the renaissance of Swedish cinema that took place in the 1940s; on the other hand, Ekman's films are often engaged in a critical dialogue with Swedish society, and in order to fully appreciate them the wider context is important.

There are two things worth pointing out about Swedish cinema history. The first is that Swedish cinema has a good reputation and has received much attention from film scholars. The silent era, often seen as a golden age, has been substantially written about, as have the 1960s and beyond. But there are still gaps, and one gap in particular stands out. In his book *Ingmar Bergman: Magician and Prophet* (1999), Marc Gervais points out that very little is known of, and consequently written about, Swedish cinema between 1924 and 1945, the years following Victor Sjöström and Mauritz Stiller's departure to Hollywood but prior to Ingmar Bergman's début as a director, and that this is a problem (Gervais 1999: 24). To give a few examples, in David Bordwell and Kristin Thompson's *Film History – An Introduction* (2003), Swedish cinema between 1924 and 1944 is not mentioned at all; neither is it mentioned in Mark Cousins's *The Story of Film* (2004), nor in David A. Cook's *A History of Narrative Film* (2004). It seems as though the historical and critical consensus is that nothing of interest happened during those years. Yet this was a time of great progress and experimentation, which is why it is relevant to call it a renaissance. In view of the international standing and importance of Swedish cinema from the 1950s onwards, it is important to investigate and discuss the context and the special circumstances that helped give Sweden, a rather small country, such a comparatively strong profile.

The second point worth making is that Swedish cinema has been almost synonymous with Bergman, yet by placing so much emphasis on Bergman, film historians have ended up with a skewed view of both Bergman and Swedish cinema. A second, more implicit, aim of this book is therefore to contribute to a much needed contextualisation of Bergman, especially those early years in the 1940s during which he gradually became a filmmaker of international standing. Whereas there is a large number of books about Bergman, in many different languages, there is very little written about Hasse Ekman in any language. He has received only a few sentences in English-language books about Swedish film history in general. But what is more remarkable is how little is written about Hasse Ekman in Swedish, and how narrow the focus is of that which has been written. For example, Ekman's career as a filmmaker lasted for twenty-five years but only the first twelve years have been discussed by historians and scholars, along with only a small selection of the films. And hardly anything is written about the last half of his career. This book is the first comprehensive discussion and analysis of Ekman's complete body of work that has ever been undertaken, in any language.

One article about Ekman, by Cecilia Axelsson, has mentioned auteur studies, but her conclusion was that Ekman's oeuvre was eclectic, that it did not have any recurring themes, that it was hard to find a common thread or a personal touch, and that he did not seem hospitable to auteur studies because he did not fit such a model (Axelsson 1995). This book makes the exact opposite argument.

As has been mentioned, Ekman was virtually forgotten after he made his last film but occasionally he has been 'discovered'. The first 'discovery' of Ekman's films came in 1982 when Bengt Forslund wrote *Från Gösta Ekman till Gösta Ekman – en bok om Hasse, far och son* (1982, From Gösta Ekman to Gösta Ekman – a Book about Hasse, Father and Son). In this piece of popular film history, Forslund's aim was to look at the Ekman family and in particular Gösta Ekman and his grandson Gösta (Hasse's son), a popular actor in Sweden since the 1960s. It does not cover Swedish cinema in detail or offer much insight into Ekman's Sweden, but it says more about Hasse Ekman than any other book, except Leif Furhammar (and Jannike Åhlund)'s *En liten bok om Hasse* (1993, A Little Book about Hasse). Furhammar is a leading Swedish film historian and in this short book he discusses twelve of Ekman's most important films. The book also has a long interview with Ekman, conducted by Jannike Åhlund. It was the second 'discovery' of Ekman and it came out in conjunction with a retrospective of Ekman's films at the international film festival in Göteborg, in the south-west of Sweden. Ekman also wrote two autobiographical books. The most relevant is *Den vackra ankungen* (1955, The Handsome Duckling) in which he looked back at his film career up to that point. The other one was written when Ekman was only seventeen and is called *Hur ska det gå för mig?* (1933, What Will Happen to Me?).

These are the only books that focus on Hasse Ekman. In addition, there are a few articles in film journals and a couple of dissertations but since they add nothing new they are of minor interest (though they will be mentioned again in later chapters). However, there are various books on Swedish cinema in general in which Hasse Ekman figures. Among them is Furhammar's seminal *Filmen i Sverige* (1991, Cinema in Sweden). It is the standard work on Swedish cinema history and Swedish cinema culture and it covers every detail from the late nineteenth century to the present day. It discusses film politics and studios, genres and directors, actors and producers, the business side and the national side. Like the above-mentioned books, it is only available in Swedish.

Among the few books in English that mention Ekman are *Nordic National Cinema* (1998) by Tytti Soila, Astrid Söderbergh Widding and Gunnar Iversen; *The Cinema of Scandinavia* (2005), edited by Tytti Soila; and *Swedish Film – An Introduction and Reader* (2010), edited by Mariah Larsson and Anders Marklund. *Nordic National Cinema* begins and ends with discussions on various aspects of national cinema as such, and in between are longer essays on the film history of each of the five Nordic countries. Soila has written the essay that deals with

Swedish cinema. It moves swiftly through one hundred years of film history and even though there is not much on Ekman, she covers many angles, from production conditions to actors. *The Cinema of Scandinavia* consists of twenty-four essays, each about a specific film from one of the three Scandinavian countries and Finland. What is of most interest here is a chapter by Astrid Söderbergh Widding about *The Fire-Bird* (*Eldfågeln*, 1952), a ballet film directed by Ekman. The chapter places the film in the context of Swedish cinema in the early 1950s and the particular historical circumstances of that time. *Swedish Film – An Introduction and Reader* is an overview of Swedish cinema from its inception until the present day. In brief chapters various aspects, such as censorship, distribution, specific filmmakers and genres, are discussed. There is also a chapter on one of Ekman's most famous films, *Girl with Hyacinths* (*Flicka och hyacinter*, 1950). That chapter unfortunately lacks much historical context.

Among other books on Swedish cinema in English is *Swedish Cinema, from Ingeborg Holm to Fanny and Alexander* (1987) by Peter Cowie. It is an introduction to Swedish cinema and Swedish cinema history, from the beginnings to the early 1980s. It touches only the surface, with film history presented as a succession of one director after another, and the 1930s and 1940s together are given only fifteen pages out of a total of 150. There is also Brian McIlroy's *World Cinema 2: Sweden* (1986), which offers a concise summary of Swedish film history. There are, of course, a very substantial number of books about Ingmar Bergman but if they engage at all with Swedish cinema and society in any comprehensible manner it is in the decades after those covered in this book. Hardly any book about Bergman acknowledges the presence of Ekman, other than his performances in three of Bergman's films, with one exception: Paisley Livingston's *Cinema, Philosophy, Bergman* (2009), which mentions Ekman as a filmmaker comparable to Bergman. In *Cinema Borealis: Ingmar Bergman and the Swedish Ethos* (1971), Vernon Young dismisses Ekman with one sentence: 'Hasse Ekman made an uncertain beginning with a war film, a political film, and a gloomy drama which in point of departure resembled Noel Coward's *Brief Encounter*, filmed two years later by David Lean, before settling into a sequence of films largely inspired by deviated mental behaviour' (Young 1971: 25). This sentence gets the facts wrong and does not do Ekman justice; there is much more to Ekman than Young suggested.

Ekman was not only a filmmaker; he was also a theatre director. Here the lack of critical material is even more striking. As far as it has been possible to establish, no books, not even general books on Swedish theatre history, deal with Ekman's theatre years. Also, since it is not possible today to witness his staging of the plays it is very difficult to discuss them. However, when appropriate his theatre career will be invoked here because it is important and cannot be ignored. It is important both because his theatre work took up a large part of his career and because he made many films that are about the theatre and the people who work in theatre. This is a recurring theme and milieu throughout Ekman's whole oeuvre.

When discussing the work of a specific filmmaker it is of course important to present the context in which he or she is working, for several reasons. In the first place it emphasises that any artist or filmmaker works in a particular time and place, and not in a vacuum. Such a context may further explain why it was that particular films were made at a particular time; that is, with ample attention to the social, economic and cultural circumstances. The context is also important for a proper understanding of Ekman's themes. An additional function of this context is to make clear that both Bergman and Ekman were part of a larger movement in Swedish cinema, which included many other filmmakers – as well as producers, cinematographers and actors – several of whom were also important and inter-esting, for reasons that will be explained at length. So the approach to studying the films of Hasse Ekman has been twofold: to view Ekman's films as a coherent oeuvre, and to define and explain what the key elements of this body of work are, what defines him as an auteur, and simultaneously to place him and his films in a national context. To further both these aims there will be an engagement with the writings of film critics who were Ekman's contemporaries. Since so little has been written about Ekman by film historians, these critical opinions provide important insights into how he was discussed in his own time. Invoking the critics also serves the purpose of highlighting the fact that Ekman was considered a major filmmaker, one of the very best that Sweden had, which makes the lack of scholarly interest all the more surprising.

The first chapter will discuss some theoretical assumptions regarding author-ship and national cinema. The following two chapters will look at the Swedish context, the first in terms of politics and the second in terms of film culture and the film industry. The next three chapters, 4, 5 and 6, will look at Ekman's career, chronologically, and discuss themes, motifs and stylistic preferences with refer-ence to individual films and to the context in which they were made. Chapter 7 will provide a specific discussion of Ekman's worldview and his relationship to Sweden. Several of the written works that are quoted in subsequent chapters have only been published in Swedish and the translations here are my own. That is also the case with quoted dialogue from Swedish films. When a quotation from a written work has been translated, this will be indicated with 'trans.'. Many of the films mentioned do not have an English or international title. Here they have all been given English titles, with the original title given the first time the film is mentioned.

CHAPTER 1

On Auteurs and National Cinema

Although discussing the films of Hasse Ekman within the context of Swedish national cinema, this is primarily a straightforward study of an auteur. The main reason for this approach is that this is the first English-language study of Ekman's films, and should therefore cover all the films with which he was involved, focusing on his particular contribution to them and to Swedish cinema in general. This study will provide a foundation for further discussions of individual films and aspects of his career from various theoretical standpoints and towards the end of the book there will be suggestions for other angles from which to continue to explore and analyse Ekman's body of work.

But since the concept of auteurs, or auteurism, is much contested would it not be better to disregard it? Some believe so and consider it a romantic delusion, or obsolete in the context of contemporary cinema studies. As Catherine Grant has argued, 'film authorship has rarely been considered a wholly legitimate object of contemplation' (Grant 2000: 101). So is the term 'auteur' really necessary? Is not cinema a collaborative art form? Might not the word 'filmmaker' suffice instead, or perhaps just 'director', as they are not questioned in the same way as 'auteur' is? But there is a difference between 'filmmaker', 'director' and 'auteur'. A person who makes educational films, or public relations films, is a filmmaker but hardly ever an auteur. A director likewise. A director might not have had a hand in the development of the script but an auteur almost always has. And it is precisely because cinema is a collaborative art form that it is relevant to speak about auteurs. Films are made by a number of people but they are not all of equal importance for the finished result.

Thinking about auteurs is not new with regards to filmmaking: it was happening almost right at the beginning of film history, even though it is sometimes assumed that it first came about in the mid-1950s. The following section will emphasise this historical background, and also specify the way in which 'auteur' is defined and used in this book, precisely because it is a contested term and has been defined in many different ways.

When talking about authorship and auteurs it is customary to begin in France in the 1950s with the writings of Alexandre Astruc, André Bazin, François Truffaut,

Jean-Luc Godard and others. *Film History – An Introduction* (Bordwell & Thompson 2003: 415–417), *The Film Experience – An Introduction* (Corrigan & White 2009: 465–466) and *Approaches to Popular Film* (Hollows & Jancovich 1995: 37–58) are examples of books that place the emergence of ideas about directors as auteurs in France at this time. But this is to some extent ahistorical since already by the beginning of the twentieth century there was a particular focus on the director in cinema. Traditionally, film has been seen as the director's medium, not least from a marketing perspective. The poster for the US film *Intolerance* (1916) is an example of this. Despite the fact that some of Hollywood's most famous stars at the time, such as Lillian Gish and Mae Marsh, acted in the film, the name used to sell it was that of its director, D.W. Griffith. The poster also makes a direct reference to a previous film by Griffith. The words on the poster, directly below the film title, are 'Mr Griffith's first production since "The Birth of a Nation"'. Using only the name of the director, however, was still rather unusual. Usually, the director and the names of some of the more famous actors would be used, such as on the poster for the first version of *Ben-Hur: A Tale of the Christ* (1925): the name of the director, Fred Niblo, comes first, and in slightly bigger letters than the names of the actors. For a typical Swedish example, the poster for *The Phantom Carriage* (*Körkarlen*, 1921) is illustrative. Beneath a drawing of the eponymous carriage it reads: 'Selma Lagerlöf's *The Phantom Carriage* told in moving images by Victor Sjöström' (trans.). The selling point was definitely the authors behind it: Lagerlöf, who wrote the short story, and Sjöström, who directed the film. On the poster for Hasse Ekman's first film, *With You in My Arms* (*Med dej i mina armar*, 1940) it says 'Direction: Hasse Ekman' (trans.) as an enticement to the audience.

These examples have focused mainly on the marketing perspective and it should also be added that film trailers often used the director's name as a selling point, the director sometimes even appearing in the trailer. Of course, it was not only the publicity departments that were promoting the director above other members of the crew. In early film theory, films were also often attributed to their directors, as in this passage by Jean Epstein written in the 1920s:

> But the proper sensibility, by which I mean a personal one, can direct the lens towards increasingly valuable discoveries. This is the role of an author of film, commonly called a film director. Of course a landscape filmed by one of the forty or four hundred directors devoid of personality whom God sent to plague the cinema as He once sent the locusts into Egypt looks exactly like this same

landscape filmed by any other of these locust filmmakers. But this landscape or this fragment of drama staged by someone like Gance will look nothing like what would be seen through the eyes and heart of a Griffith or a L'Herbier. And so the personality, the soul, the poetry of certain men invaded the cinema. (Epstein 1988: 317–318)

Since Epstein was writing in French, he of course used the word *auteur*, which here was translated into 'author'. He unequivocally equates the author with the director, and for him this is an important aspect of what makes cinema an art form.

Another theorist writing in the 1920s, Louis Delluc, wrote about the director as the unifying force and argued that the director, if he is good enough, is the genius behind the film and is even, if he is as brilliant as Thomas Ince, capable of creating a masterpiece out of nothing (cited in McCreary 1976). Vachel Lindsay is yet another early example of a theorist who championed the notion of the 'auteur' (Lindsay 2000). One of Britain's leading twentieth-century film critics, Dilys Powell, had what might be called an auteurist approach, at least from the beginning of the 1930s. When she wrote, in the 1930s and 1940s, about individual films by the likes of Carol Reed, Alfred Hitchcock, John Ford and Fritz Lang, she frequently discussed those films as being part of each director's larger body of work. In 1946 she talked about the national, industrial and cooperative aspects of cinema and then asked the rhetorical question: 'How can one man leave the mark of his personality and his talent on this hugger-mugger?' and she answered, 'But he does' (Powell 1991: 37). In Sweden in the early 1940s there was a debate among film critics and scholars about who should be considered the true author of a film. There were those who said that it should be the writer and those who said it should be the director. In a summary of the debate the critic Georg Svensson came down firmly on the side of the director (Svensson 1941), in an article that would not have been out of place in an issue of *Cahiers du cinéma*, some fifteen years later.

In other words, directors, since the early days of cinema, have often been seen as the main force behind a film, the artist making it, by both critics and theorists. And the publicity departments used the name of the director as a selling point, which seems to suggest that for the public too it was the director who counted most, together with the actors. These ideas were then amplified in the 1950s and 1960s, especially in France (*Cahiers du cinéma*), in the UK (from 1962 in *Movie*) and in the USA, especially through the writings of the critic Andrew Sarris. At this point, it came to be known as the 'auteur theory'. However, it should be stressed that, although often used, the term 'auteur theory' is questionable. Even Sarris, who wrote extensively about it and helped make the idea popular in the US, said that it was not a theory as such and that: '[u]ltimately the auteur theory is not so much a theory as an attitude' (Sarris 1968: 30). It is rather a critical approach, or, as Robert Stam would have it, a 'methodological focus' (Stam 2000: 91). In this study the term *auteurism* is used instead.

The strong reactions against the idea of the auteur, and authors in general, emerged especially in the late 1960s and the 1970s (see for example Heath 1973; Foucault 1977; Kael 2007). Some of the criticism came from structuralists and post-structuralists, who argued that the author is not important but should be seen as merely a mediator between the text and the audience (Stam 2000: 123–125). The author might even, as in Roland Barthes's famous essay from 1967, be declared dead. Barthes is concerned with language, which for him is the central creator of meaning: 'it is language which speaks, not the author' (Barthes 1977: 143). By 'killing off' the author, as it were, the text is liberated and becomes open to the reader's own ideas and interpretations, and in a sense the text is created when it is being read. However, three years later Barthes opened up the possibility that the author might actually be alive in the text. In the essay 'From Work to Text' he wrote that: 'It is not that the Author may not "come back" in the Text, in his text, but he then does so as a "guest". If he is a novelist, he is inscribed in the novel like one of his characters' (Barthes 1977: 161). When Barthes wrote about films his writing was usually focused on the director, his skills and intentions. In an article in *Le Monde* about the film *French Provincial* (*Souvenirs d'en France*, André Téchiné, 1975) Barthes wrote: 'With Téchiné comes lightness: this is a significant event not just for the theory of film-making but also for the practice of film-watching' (quoted in Calvet 1994: 193). This seems to suggest not only that the author is alive, but also that the director is significant. Barthes has also written, favourably, about Sergei Eisenstein, Charles Chaplin and others (Barthes 1994), so maybe the auteur never was dead, not even for Barthes.

In the article by Catherine Grant mentioned earlier she emphasises towards the end that the auteur will not go away, and that there are good reasons for this. She mentions for example the importance of auteurs within cinephilia and also how minorities, be it sexual or ethnic, have stressed the importance of gay filmmakers, filmmakers with immigrant backgrounds or members of some other minority group. 'An academic commerce in auteurism, then, continues apace, hardly touched by the earlier debates, except perhaps that many more previously marginal auteurial "subjects" are invited for discussion (women, gays, non-white, non-western filmmakers, and so on)' (Grant 2000: 108).

In recent times Dorothy Arzner, an early female filmmaker in the Hollywood studio system (when it was very rare to find women in such a position), is one of many who have been 'discovered' (see, for instance, Johnston 1975); another example of this trend is Christina Lane's research on the writer/producer Joan Harrison (Lane 2003). There are also now several studies of queer filmmakers, such as Michael DeAngelis' work on Todd Haynes within New Queer Cinema (DeAngelis 2006). Such work points to the relevance of auteur studies from a perspective of equality and progressiveness or what James Naremore refers to as 'an attack on convention and a form of resistance'. He also argues that auteur studies have the ability to explore, expand and challenge canons and previous thinking about film history (Naremore 2014: 31–32) and that idea is partly what inspired this study of Hasse Ekman.

Today there is a common expression in film criticism which has taken the notion of the auteur to a different level. It is the expression 'auteur cinema'. In a way it is the opposite of traditional auteurism, even though the terms are frequently used synonymously. 'Auteur cinema' is often put in opposition to commercial cinema, and by doing so the difference between 'auteur cinema' and traditional auteurism becomes clear, since auteurists, such as Andrew Sarris, were arguing that there was no contradiction between auteurs and commercial cinema and that auteurs were in fact plentiful in commercial cinema. So 'auteur cinema' is an unhelpful term. It is often used as a marketing device at film festivals and by arthouse cinemas to distinguish their films from the mainstream cinema, as if mainstream cinema could not possess auteurs. It is sometimes said against auteurism that it is a romantic idea, as when Linda Haverty Rugg argues that the concept of the auteur is 'imbued with romantic notions of artistic genius' (Rugg 2005: 228–229). That is a valid criticism of the concept of 'auteur cinema', because it suggests films that are made by creative geniuses beyond genres and commerce. But it is not a valid criticism against auteurs as such, in the way that the concept is used in this book.

Films can be analysed from an economic perspective, an industrial perspective or an audience perspective. But, whilst important, such perspectives will not fully explain why a particular, individual film was made and neither will it explain what the particular circumstances were in which that film was made. This is something important that auteurism brings to the study of cinema. Part of history and its progress are ideas and emotions, and these originate in human beings. This is naturally true for film history as well. By not discussing the actual people making the films, an important part of film history goes missing, and it will not be possible to gain a complete understanding of that history. In the introduction to his book on Luchino Visconti, Geoffrey Nowell-Smith writes:

> As a principle of method the [auteur] theory requires the critic to recognize the basic fact, which is that the author exists, and to organize his analysis of the work around that fact. Whether one is trying to get to grips with a particular film, or to understand the cinema in general, let alone when one is studying the development of an individual director, the concept of authorship provides a necessary dimension without which the picture cannot be complete. ... [O]ne essential corollary of the theory as it has been developed is the discovery that the defining characteristics of an author's work are not always those that are most readily apparent. (Nowell-Smith 2003: 10)

The key point here is that 'the author exists'. S/he is not something that can be theorised away. Films are made by individuals, individuals who think, act and make conscious decisions: they are independent agents, and to quote Torben Grodal, 'It is fundamental for normal human functioning that our theory of other minds acknowledges that such minds belong to conscious, intending, and desiring beings' (Grodal 2004: 15).

However, there are more agents than just directors on a film set and the automatic focus on the director can be problematic. Scriptwriters and cinematographers tend to be overlooked, as well as other contributors. It is quite obvious, for example, how Michael Powell has been given much more attention than Emeric Pressburger, despite the fact that they worked as an intimate team. (Interestingly, there are a number of such teams in British cinema. Other examples are the Boulting Brothers, Basil Dearden/Michael Relph and Frank Launder/Sidney Gilliat.) In *Our Films, Their Films* Satyajit Ray wrote:

> A director weak on the visual side may be considerably helped by a cameraman with a sense of drama. When a director is a true auteur – that is, if he controls every aspect of production – then the cameraman is obliged to perform an interpretative role. Whenever he does more than that, the director should humbly part with some of his credit as an auteur. (Ray 1994: 68)

This seems only reasonable, and not only with regard to the camera operator, but also with scriptwriters, set designers and composers. Paul Coates calls these other participants 'mini-*auteurs*' (Coates 1985: 83). The critic and the scholar should see to it that credit is shared, stressing the importance of co-workers and companions, of writers, cinematographers, producers and actors, in the making of the films being considered. Even so in most cases the director is still the central force on the set – the person who is responsible for the whole of the film. As V.F. Perkins wrote in *Film as Film*, 'The director's authority is a matter not of total creation but of sufficient control' (Perkins 1993: 184); the word 'control' being important. As a writer, producer and director, as well as an actor, Ekman had considerable control, as shall be seen later. On the other hand, it is hard to judge how much control each individual has had on a film set without actually having been there to observe. That is why it is important to stress that with the approach taken in this book, the study of a larger body of work is essential. If there are clear links between the films of a particular filmmaker this strongly suggests that the filmmaker had at least some measure of control over how they were made. It is argued here that whether the filmmaker in question worked as a contracted studio director or as an independent filmmaker is not what decides his or her status as auteur. It is the consistency and cohesiveness of their oeuvre that matters in this definition. This empirical approach to auteurism means that most, if not all, films of the individual filmmaker under investigation should be watched. Additionally, films made by many other filmmakers working at the same time, and before, should also be analysed in order to be able to pick out what it is that makes this particular body of work special, and to be able to see the unique contributions made by a particular auteur. This book further argues that there is a difference between 'director' and 'auteur' in the sense that 'director' is a job title, describing a person from the moment they start to work on the film set, whereas with the definition of an auteur used in this study it is not meaningful to say of a first-time director that s/he is an auteur. A larger body of work that can be analysed as a whole is needed.

Another difficult question, besides the cooperative aspects of filmmaking, and one which is perhaps an integral part of the discussion of authors and authorship, is the autobiographical aspect. Links between an artist's work and his/her own personal life and history have been made repeatedly over the ages. It is common enough either to consciously look for the connections between a character (in a book or film) and the artist, or to compare specific events or actions in the artist's past with specific events or actions in the artwork. However, one potential problem with looking for such links is the autobiographical fallacy. Any work of fiction, regardless of how closely linked it may appear to be to the artist's life, is still a processed story, where things have been altered and manipulated. Sometimes this is done simply to better fit the narrative structure and sometimes it is done in a deliberate effort to change the reader's or viewer's perception of what really happened. The artist might, for example, overplay dramatic events in order to evoke sympathy or give a narrative a happy ending which in real life ended tragically. What the artist says about his/her work may also be part of that process of alteration and manipulation. A correlation between a character in a film and the actual filmmaker does not necessarily mean they are the same person. However, it is not the case that autobiographical readings should be dismissed out of hand. It is close to impossible to create a narrative without using, consciously or unconsciously, real-life experiences and putting them into the story, the structure. Here it is also important to consider the fact that even if an artist vehemently denies that there is anything autobiographical in their work, that should not be taken at face value either. They may not want to admit it, or may fail to see it, even though the biographical aspects might still be there, and obvious for someone else. While acknowledging these concerns, in this book there will be autobiographical readings of some of Ekman's films. (For discussions on autobiographical readings, see Mazierska & Rascaroli (2004) or Staiger (2008).)

The history of film is filled with auteurs and to make the discussion more precise, distinctions between different kinds of auteurs are helpful. I would like to propose a new one, the distinction between *external auteurs* and *internal auteurs*. An *external auteur* would be somebody who simply makes films yet has no presence in them, even though the films have thematic and stylistic consistencies and recurring motifs. An *internal auteur* would be somebody who, besides making the films, has a strong presence in them, either personally and/or through a voice-over and/or by including strong autobiographical elements in the film. External auteurs are more common, for instance Henry Hathaway or Gillian Armstrong. Internal auteurs are not as common, but among the more prominent in narrative cinema are Rainer Werner Fassbinder, Federico Fellini, Chantal Akerman, Clint Eastwood, Orson Welles, François Truffaut, Woody Allen, Ida Lupino, Alfred Hitchcock and Ingmar Bergman. Their strong personal presence in the films they made can lead to difficulties in interpreting their work, especially in separating filmmaker, character and actor, but these filmmakers can also be especially rewarding to analyse, and they can serve as a counterpoint to theories that diminish the role of the filmmaker, such as Barthes's. Hasse Ekman should be considered an internal auteur, and to an extent not usually found outside of avant-garde cinema. Besides writing, directing and acting in his own films, and even playing the part based on himself in those of his films that have autobiographical elements, he sometimes also does a voice-over. This intermingling of different roles for Ekman (the director, the writer, the subject of the story and the actor in the film) can sometimes become rather complex and will be further discussed.

The difficulties with reading films autobiographically are emphasised when it comes to internal auteurs. So too are the temptations of understanding the films as just that: autobiographical 'truths' in some sense. However, research beyond simply watching the films, such as reading interviews, archival material or autobiographies, is needed in order to establish to what extent a particular film is autobiographical, and whether that is important.

Ekman can be seen as a combination of a classical and a modernist filmmaker. *Classical* often refers to Hollywood cinema, especially before the 1960s, involving story-based, as opposed to character-based, narratives told in a linear fashion and with a clear-cut ending that does not leave any loose ends, and where there is no breaking of the fourth wall, such as direct address to the audience by the actors. *Modernist* typically refers to the post-war European art film, involving character-based narratives and loose endings with a more experimental attitude to style and context. This is also sometimes called art-cinema narrative (see Bordwell 1985). This distinction has always been fraught and the differences are often more apparent than real, as there were plenty of modernist ideas and impulses in pre-1960s Hollywood cinema as well as post-1960, and many films in post-war Europe can equally be seen as 'classical'. So, since the distinction in general is too simplistic, it would be better to talk about individual films as being classical or modernist, rather than establishing a dichotomy between classical cinema (such as Hollywood cinema) on the one hand and modernist cinema (such as European post-war cinema) on the other hand. Ekman's films are a mix of some that are more classic and some that are more modernist; however, the use of character-based narratives, open endings, self-reflexivity and autobiographical elements is prevalent right from the beginning of his career. There are many examples, as will be illustrated later on.

To recapitulate, in the context of this book auteurism is seen as an empirical way of looking for patterns in the oeuvre of a filmmaker. To be as clear as possible, it will rest on the following assumptions:

(1) All narrative films are created by individuals, working alone or in collaboration.
(2) These individuals are independent agents who can hence be considered as authors and artists.
(3) Auteurs are creators, be they directors, writers, producers or cinematographers, who over a body of work show thematic and/or stylistic consistencies.
(4) The cinema studies approach which searches for, and discusses, these consistencies is called auteurism.
(5) Auteurism is an empirical approach, and a way, among many others, of trying to understand cinema history.
(6) There are different kinds of auteurs, and a distinction is made in this book between external and internal auteurs.
(7) Auteurism should preferably be used in conjunction with other approaches, to put the subject being studied in a proper context.
(8) Auteurism is not an evaluative approach, and has nothing to do with 'good' or 'bad' cinema. It stands outside notions of 'commercial cinema', 'art cinema', 'independent cinema' and other evaluative stances.

The author does not appear out of nowhere or work in a vacuum; s/he is part of a larger context. That context can be regional, national or global, but here it is the national that is the chosen context. Swedish cinema has a history of explicitly engaging with, and even exploiting, national specifics in film production. With reference to the Swedish cinema of the 1910s and early 1920s, David Bordwell and Kristin Thompson argue that: 'Sweden was among the first countries to create a major cinema by drawing deliberately on the particular traits of its national culture' (Bordwell & Thompson 2003: 64). Leif Furhammar continues with this Swedish national discourse when he argues that in the Swedish cinema of the 1930s a major theme in most of the films was to project a sense of national belonging, to instil in the audience a sense of togetherness under the Swedish welfare state (Furhammar 1991: 161). He then goes on to argue that this more or less disappeared in the 1940s. Since Ekman began making films in 1940, he was part of this new, less nationalistic generation of filmmakers.

However, the concept of a 'national' cinema is problematic. Is it really possible, or even relevant, to sum up all films made by a particular nation and analyse them as a whole? It would by default lead to simplifications and generalisations. At the same time, if the sample is too small, it will be impossible to tell how representative the chosen films are of the nation which produced them. It would also entail a very clear definition of that nation. Tom O'Regan asks, in his influential work *Australian National Cinema* (1996), if one should call 'the growing body [in Australia] of short films shot in Italian, Spanish and Greek a contribution to the Italian, Spanish and Greek "national cinemas" or ... "Australian cinema"'. He further asks if a discussion about Australian cinema should include or exclude films made by aboriginal nations living within the Australian state (O'Regan 1996: 74). Such a discussion is also relevant for a scholar working with Swedish cinema. From the 1930s to the 1950s, Sweden was not a multicultural country and was not a destination for immigrants; rather it was a country which had lost over a million citizens through massive emigration, mostly to the USA and Australia (Hofsten & Lundström 1976). After Norway gained its independence from Sweden in 1905, Sweden was fairly homogeneous, albeit with strong class divisions. However, it could be argued that it was not a proper nation-state since there lived within Sweden's borders the indigenous Sami people, and there has been an ongoing struggle between them and the rest of the population. The Sami people might be considered a nation without a state, dispersed as they are among several Nordic states and Russia. It is not the purpose of this book to engage in debates on these matters, only to offer a glimpse of what constituted 'Sweden' in the 1940s and 1950s, and show that Sweden encompasses different nations.

Another problem is the risk of essentialism. In his book on the Taiwanese filmmaker Hou Hsiao-Hsien, James Udden highlights this danger and talks about the Orientalist view many scholars have taken when discussing Hou's films: their efforts to 'explain' him and his films by reference to the fact that he is from Taiwan (Udden 2009: 1–8). The same mistake is often made when Bergman is discussed. The bleakness the critics see in Bergman's films is explained by, or seen as an example of, his Swedish-ness or Scandinavian-ness. It is not usually explained why Sweden or Scandinavia is, or should be, associated with something bleak, or which parts of the Scandinavian region are being referred to. It would also seem to suggest that all those Swedish filmmakers whose works are not bleak or austere are somehow less Swedish than Bergman.

Studies of national cinema usually involve case studies of state funding of the films of that particular nation. This adds an additional 'national' element to the films. In the films and the era discussed in this book, however, there was no state funding. All films were funded by the production companies or the filmmakers themselves and there were no national initiatives or institutions to support and assist the films into production. Such public assistance came later. If anything, the government at times rather hindered the development of the cinema, as will be discussed later.

Having considered these problems with national cinema, there are still ways of using the national context when discussing films and film history. Writing on national cinema, Andrew Higson has argued that there are four uses of the term:

- an economic sense (a production and industrial perspective);
- an audience perspective (Who is watching the films and how do they interpret them?);
- a marketing perspective (the nation as a brand); and
- the perspective of representation (What values or ideas are projected in, and through, the films?). (Higson 1995: 4–6)

With regard to Ekman, the first use is taken for granted; his films were financed and made in Sweden. The second use of the term is not applicable here. For the aims of this book, looking at the films from the perspective of an audience is not necessary. The third use, the marketing perspective, is not relevant here either. In some Swedish films, especially of the 1930s, there was a conscious effort to build up a national brand, to sell Swedish-ness to the Swedish spectators, and this will be duly discussed later in the book, but Ekman was not involved in this 'brand-building'. Higson's fourth use is closer to what this book is concerned with, which will be explained later in this chapter.

A key question when discussing an artist in a national context is: Could this artist have done this same work of art in another country? An equally relevant question is: Is the nation that produced this particular film reflected in it? Sometimes the nation is without importance, it is just present, whereas at other times the nation is central to the story of the film. Different filmmakers will work differently in this respect. Some directors, for example Theo Angelopoulos, make films specifically about their own countries, be it either from a celebratory or a critical perspective, to the extent that the themes of the films are intimately connected with nationalism, the nation and its history – in Angelopoulos's case, Greece (see, for example, Horton (1997)). This is not the case with Ekman. Ekman's films were produced in Sweden, and in general they take place in Stockholm, the capital of Sweden, but in several films the nation is not relevant:

it is accidental, in the sense that the film just happens to be made in that place. Such films might be called 'a-national'. However, whilst many of the characters and stories may be of a more urban than national significance, the films are still made by Swedes and set in Sweden, so it would be hard, perhaps impossible, for them to be completely removed from the particular Swedish context. As will be discussed in chapter 4, one essential aspect of Ekman's films is the dialogue: the language which the characters speak and how Ekman plays with words, sentences and dialects. Language could be seen as a defining national trait, especially with films made in a language which is spoken in only one country. If a spectator did not know where the film s/he was watching came from, recognising the language might be the first clue as to the nationality of the film (at least in countries where dubbing is not used). With the complex transnational financial arrangements behind many films, especially if the locations are spread out among several countries, or if the locations are not known, then the language spoken by the actors might even be the spectator's *only* clue to its nationality. It is not only language that matters but also dialects or accents of a language, as in Australian, British or American English. So with regard to language, Ekman's films are unquestionably Swedish, and can therefore unequivocally be defined as such. From a financial perspective too, Ekman's films are Swedish since the money for making them came from Swedish sources. (The exceptions are two European co-productions, *Waiting Room for Death* aka *Interlude* (*I dödens väntrum*, 1946) and *The Fire-Bird*, which both have international settings and international casts, and which are bi- or even trilingual.) In addition to the language and financial factors, the films Ekman made were constrained by certain factors peculiar to Sweden, such as censorship rules, especially during the Second World War. There were also other political and economic factors that were peculiar to Sweden, and these factors will be discussed later.

Some of Ekman's films also engage directly with certain aspects of Swedish society (the place of women and how society is organised are aspects that Ekman occasionally focusses upon). The view of these particular aspects of Swedish society that comes across in the films is often ambivalent but even more often critical. So even if many of Ekman's films do not directly engage with the nation, the nation is still there and even if not discussing Ekman's films as 'national cinema', it is still possible to look at how the national context in which they were made influenced them. The look of Ekman's films will also be compared with that of other Swedish films made at that time.

To summarise, the approach taken here is to look at Ekman's films as a complete body of work and to describe and analyse this body of work from an auteurist perspective, while situating it in a specific national context. This is intended to highlight both this particular filmmaker and this context.

CHAPTER 2

The Social Context

This chapter will present, in chronological order, some important aspects of Swedish history from the early 1930s to the mid-1960s, and introduce Swedish society, politics, economics and culture. This is not merely because of the need for some political background, but also because these were the years during which Ekman came of age and started to work, and because this period is sometimes reflected in his films. Consideration of the 1930s is vital, therefore, for a broader understanding of both Sweden and Ekman, and not least the introduction of the term *folkhemmet*. This word is an essential part of Sweden's history and its sense of itself, and also affects Ekman's films and how they were seen by critics and scholars. So even though there are not always direct references to Ekman in this chapter, the historical circumstances discussed are central to a proper understanding of his work and his themes.

Democracy in Sweden began to take shape in the late nineteenth century and by 1921, when women won the right to vote, it was fully established. As referred to earlier, Sweden had been, and still was, a net-emigrant country, which means that more people moved out of the country than moved in. This was primarily due to widespread poverty. It was not an egalitarian country and there were many who lived in abject poverty, in almost slave-like conditions. From the mid-1700s all the way until 1945 there was in Sweden a system whereby the owner of a mansion hired married people for one-year contracts, so-called *statare*, in which they were often not paid with money but with food and housing, and had to live in special shacks (called *statarlängor*). They had few rights and were at the mercy of their employers. Various films, such as *Karl Fredrik Reigns* (*Karl Fredrik regerar*, Gustaf Edgren, 1934) and *The Emigrants* (*Utvandrarna*, Jan Troell, 1971), deal with this issue.

But the industrial revolution, which came to Sweden in the middle of the nineteenth century and lasted until the First World War, brought on a sharp increase in wealth and growth and wages rose accordingly (Magnusson 2002 301–310). This and increased public awareness had already begun to make change apparent by the beginning of the twentieth century, when a series of reforms took place. The 1920s saw the international breakthrough of companies such as ASEA (today ABB), SKF, Ericsson and Atlas Copco. At the same time a system whereby the workers were given grants in order to purchase their own homes was introduced. Overall, the years from 1921 until 1932 saw a very volatile labour market and those years were also politically unstable, with twelve different prime ministers succeeding each other. The critical situation came to a sort of apotheosis in 1931 when a violent strike in Ådalen in the north of Sweden ended when the army, called in by an overwhelmed police force, shot dead five demonstrators. The next year in the general election the Social Democratic Party won a clear majority and eventually formed a government together with the Farmers' Party, which had seen an internal rebellion and turned progressive (Hadenius 2003: 61). The leader of the Social Democratic Party, Per Albin Hansson, became prime minister. Hansson's ambition was to create a welfare state and it was he who popularised the term *folkhemmet*. *Folkhem* or *folkhemmet* means roughly 'the people's home' but perhaps a more accurate translation would be 'the people's society'. When discussing Ekman's films this term is key to understanding some of their narratives, especially since he sometimes directly criticise aspects of *folkhemmet*.

As a word, *folkhem* had been around for decades and probably originated in Germany with the word *volksheim*, which denoted public buildings meant to provide community services for everybody (see for example Björck 2008). At this point it literally meant 'the people's house', but Per Albin Hansson's use of the term referred to something bigger than just a house. It was a metaphor for the entire society. The aim for Hansson was to create a nation where people would be healthy, wealthy and happy, and the means to do this, he believed, was of course through politics and economics but also partly through scientific progress and by instilling a sense of a common agenda in all Swedes. In keeping with this model of consensus, in a deal made in 1938 in the Stockholm suburb of Saltsjöbaden, the Swedish Trade Union Confederation (SAF) and the Workers Union (LO) agreed to work together in harmony: through stability in the market the economy would grow and everybody would prosper. This consensus was called the Saltsjöbaden Spirit (Magnusson 2002: 445–449).

This was at about the same time that Franklin D. Roosevelt was launching the *New Deal* programme in the USA. In the UK, William Beveridge presented his report *Social Insurance and Allied Services* in 1942 which argued for an extensive welfare state, including the creation of a national health service; ideas which were implemented by the Labour government of Clement Attlee, beginning in 1945. So these ideas were in the air, globally. The Swedish Social Democrats were in theory influenced by the writings of Karl Marx but in reality their economic policy, under the finance minister Ernst Wigforss, was much closer to the ideas of the British economist John Maynard Keynes and the liberal Swedish economists banded together under the name 'the Stockholm School' (Magnusson 2002: 405–406). These policies included a preference for free trade; a proposal that the state, instead of taking over business, would invest in infrastructure and see to it that a vibrant private-business environment could flourish; and provision for those who were unemployed to be taken care of by the state. It has also been argued that it was neither Marx nor Keynes and the Stockholm School, but rather the concept of 'productivism' that was the guiding principle, meaning that the aim of the collective work of politicians, citizens and corporations was to synchronise and maximise production (Björck 2008: 193). The Swedish economy began to change from an industrial to a service economy (Hadenius 2003: 50) – a change that would only increase over time. It is important to remember that, contrary to popular wisdom, it was not a one-party state presided over by the Social Democratic Party, and it can be argued that it was a push-and-pull situation between that party and the Liberal Party. Whenever one side became too radical, the electorate sent a clear message (for example in opinion polls) that they did not want any revolutions but were more inclined to gradualism and stability. So the parties had to aim for the middle ground. It was during these years that Sweden began to attract much interest from the outside world for the way it was seen to effectively balance socialism and capitalism and for the way it managed to stay calm and progressive in Europe when most countries seemed either to become dictatorial or to backslide. A book such as Marquis W. Childs's *Sweden: A Middle Way* exemplifies this international interest. Representative of the book's stance is the following: 'The wisdom of the Swedes lies above all in their willingness to adjust, to compromise, to meet what appears to be reality. … In a sense they are the ultimate pragmatists, interested only in the workability of the social order' (Childs 1944: 161).

Besides *folkhemmet*, another prominent idea in Swedish society at the time was 'engineering'. Originating in the US at the turn of the century, the concept of the social engineer came to Sweden in the beginning of the twentieth century. The thinking was widespread and an international economic conference in Geneva in 1928, organised by the League of Nations, ended with a proclamation advocating 'the benefits of rationalisation and of scientific management' (Björck

2008: 125–126). Sweden was one of the countries where these ideas were put to most comprehensive use (see also Hirdman 2010). Included in this project were efforts to cut back on drinking habits. A large movement argued for a complete ban on alcohol consumption but after a public referendum it was instead decided that it would still be legal to sell and consume alcohol, but with far-reaching restrictions. The general movement of the 1930s was for a kind of socially engineered society, in which everything should be as functional and organised as possible. A new generation of architects, sociologists, designers, writers and government officials were working towards these aims, and were building houses, planning city centres, reforming schools, building roads and reforming the social safety net in an effort to make life better for everybody. As will be discussed later, such a scientisation of society was often at odds with Ekman's worldview.

The reverse of this combination of *folkhemmet* and rationalisation was a certain intolerance of those that did not fit in, such as the Sami people, or those with degenerative diseases or mental health problems. In 1922, Statens Institut för Rashygien (the Government Agency for Eugenics) was founded, and in 1934 a widespread system of forced sterilisation begun, which lasted up until 1965. In total some sixty-three thousand people were sterilised, in most cases because of their race or their psychiatric condition (Ronci 2008). In addition, there was widespread anti-Semitism, which can also be seen in popular culture, including films such as *Pettersson & Bendel* (Per-Axel Branner, 1933). These are among the reasons for Hans Ingvar Roth's argument that: 'The greater the proportion of social areas defined as public the less room there was for cultural idiosyncrasy in Swedish society' (Roth 2004: 222). In Ekman's films, however, there was always a celebration of this cultural idiosyncrasy, and he made some films challenging intolerance and anti-Semitism.

An important figure in most of what has been discussed so far concerning films, politics and economics was the industrial tycoon Ivar Kreuger. Kreuger was known as the matchstick king as the centre of his business empire was the making of safety matches, a business in which he had almost a global monopoly. He and his empire became extremely wealthy and expanded their influence in many fields of business. He also lent money to individual countries on such favourable terms as to contribute to the rebuilding of Europe following the First World War. This came to an end in 1932. After the Wall Street Crash of 1929 instability set in for Kreuger and it became evident that stocks and bonds were losing their value. Instead of being a creditor he had to borrow, and as things worsened he eventually shot himself in his home in Paris. That led to the 'Kreuger-crash' in Sweden, amid an atmosphere of international financial panic (Magnusson 2002: 370–372; see also Partnoy 2009).

Kreuger was also a majority owner of the leading Swedish film company Svensk Filmindustri (SF) from its inception in 1919. At that time its head of production was Charles Magnusson and this was a high point in the history of Swedish cinema. Towards the end of the 1920s, Kreuger and Magnusson had a falling out, which led to Magnusson being replaced by Olof Andersson (Furhammar 1991: 108). This was a time when the Swedish film industry was in severe crisis, but Kreuger's money kept it going through its good as well as its bad years. Fortunately for the Swedish film industry, the tide would turn and at the time of the Kreuger-crash it was no longer as dependent upon Kreuger's money as it once had been, owing to strong box-office receipts (Furhammar 1991: 138; Soila 1998: 170). In 1959, Hasse Ekman made his tribute to this era entitled *The Jazz Boy* (*Jazzgossen*, 1958).

The most important event, though, was of course the Second World War. Although official Swedish government policy was that Sweden should remain neutral, it was always adapting the policy according to the changing political circumstances, and this policy of neutrality came about after several failed attempts to form some kind of pact between the Nordic countries (Hadenius 2003: 71). After Germany and the Soviet Union signed the Molotov–Ribbentrop Pact in August 1939, which led to both countries attacking and occupying Poland, the Soviet Union turned its attention to the three Baltic states, Estonia, Latvia and Lithuania, and had soon occupied all three of them. Next came Finland, which the Red Army attacked in November 1939. This led to Per Albin Hansson forming a coalition government, including all the major parties with the exception of the Communist Party, and a declaration that Sweden was not neutral but 'non-combative'. Sweden was overtly supporting the Finnish people, even so far as to send voluntary soldiers and weapons, including fighter planes and bombers. There was a rallying call in support of the Finnish: 'Finlands sak är vår!' ('Finland's cause is our cause!'). Despite this, when the United Kingdom and France sought to send soldiers through Sweden to help Finland, the Swedish government said no (Hadenius 2003: 73–75). Sweden's position was precarious since it had to walk a thin line between Germany and the Soviet Union, and then between the Soviet Union and the West, and following that between the Allies and the Axis after the Soviet Union had aligned itself with the United States and the United Kingdom.

This outside pressure grew even stronger after Germany occupied Denmark and Norway in April 1940. So, with Germany at its borders and with a military sector which was still comparatively weak, Sweden felt that when Germany made demands for transporting troops on Swedish railways, the government had to give in, and millions of German soldiers were transferred through Swedish territory. But as the Allies, in a series of important battles, such as at El-Alamein (1942) and at Stalingrad (1942), and with the invasion of Sicily (1943), begun to gain the upper hand in the fight against Nazi Germany, and the Swedish army and air force continued to grow in strength, the government felt more secure in not giving in to German demands. Sweden also began training and arming Norwegian and Danish soldiers, and stopped selling coal and other vital raw materials to Germany.

As part of the government's early efforts to keep Sweden out of the war, and to avoid antagonising the Nazis more than necessary, the government enforced a lot of censorship, primarily of the press. In charge of the censorship was SIS, Statens Informationsstyrelse (the State Board of Information); newspapers that were considered too outspoken in their criticism of the Hitler regime were sometimes confiscated or sometimes shut down, and some journalists were sent to gaol (Gustafsson 2007). Communists were treated the same way. Films were also affected by this censorship, both with regard to which films could be imported and with regard to the subject matter of films made in Sweden, which will be dealt with in detail later in the next chapter. This applied to Ekman and his filmmaking, and censorship partly helps explain why Ekman made some of the films he did, and why he made them when he did.

The level of censorship changed over time, as the government grew less intimidated by the Germans. In October 1943, *Casablanca* (Michael Curtiz, 1942) had its Swedish premiere and caused something of a sensation since it was so overtly anti-German. But during the hard times several books appeared which, in various ways, usually allegorically, dealt with the contemporary fear of the fascism that haunted Europe. Books such as Karin Boye's *Kallocain* (1940), set in the future, Vilhelm Moberg's *Ride This Night!* (*Rid i natt,* 1941), set in the past, Pär Lagerkvist's *The Dwarf* (*Dvärgen,* 1944), an allegory about an evil man in Italy during the Renaissance, and Eyvind Johnson's Krilon trilogy (1941, 1942 and 1943) have become part of Swedish literary history. Another spokesperson with explicitly political views was the stage comedian and songwriter Karl Gerhard. He performed several anti-Nazi numbers during the war years that led to official reprimands and visits from the police. As will be discussed later, through his films Ekman was also involved in these anti-fascist activities. But war never did come explicitly to Sweden, and eventually Germany was defeated. The world celebrated and Sweden entered the post-war era.

When the war ended people were expecting a difficult time economically, with a depression as the most likely scenario. What occurred was the opposite, with pronounced growth, inflation and a huge trade deficit which led to the economy overheating. One reason for this was that Swedish infrastructure was undamaged, unlike almost any other country in Europe, and there was almost no social unrest at all (Hadenius 2003: 87). Policies continued much as they had during the war, including rationing of various items due to the trade deficit, and Sweden decided to continue its policy of neutrality. It did, however, in 1948, sign up for the Marshall Plan, the US economic support system to help rebuild Europe after the war. All of this meant that the situation for filmmakers was, for a European country at this point, unusually stable. In addition, as the war was over the strict political censorship laws disappeared.

The country became more socially liberal (homosexuality was decriminalised in 1944; abortion became legal in 1946, if there were special medical circumstances), and the economy continued to grow, moving gradually from heavy industry towards services. The electorate saw to it that neither the Liberals nor the Social Democrats became too radical, and they also kept extreme parties out of parliament, as they had almost always done (Hadenius 2003: 99). More and more women joined the workforce, and rising wages led to a fairer country, as the gap between the poor and the wealthy decreased (Magnusson 2002: 410). Among the reforms brought in were state pensions (1946) and unconditional child support (1947). In order to pay for these and other benefits, taxes were raised on a regular basis, almost doubling from 1945 to 1969 (Dahlberg 1999: 201). Ekman's films sometimes touch upon these new, progressive ideals, pushing them even further.

Sweden also became a suburban society. All over Sweden suburbs were being built and, as was often the official Swedish way of doing things, they were thoroughly planned down to every last detail. Everything was standardised in the apartment blocks – height, width, length and light – along with the entire areas in which the apartments were built. The organising principle was called ABC; A for *Arbete* (work), B for *Bostad* (apartment) and C for *Centrum* (area for doctors, dentists, restaurants, schools, shopping and cinemas), so that in theory the inhabitants would never have to leave their suburb (Dahlberg 1999: 195–196). This standardisation is commented on, and criticised, in Ekman's films, right from the beginning of his career.

Culturally, this was a time of popular successes and innovative artistic movements. Swedish design became famous, and plastic became popular. Radio and films continued to be increasingly popular, and a new generation of writers appeared, one of them being Stig Dagerman. Dagerman was a journalist, writer and occasional film critic, and he was a leading light in a group of poets and writers that were called '40-talisterna' (the 40-ists, or 'Generation 40'), so called because they all had their first works published in the 1940s. These were angst-ridden and existentialist writers, and they will be discussed later. Among the better-known members of this group, besides Dagerman, were Erik Lindegren, Karl Vennberg and Werner Aspenström. Bergman was close to this group but Ekman was not.

In the immediate aftermath of the recent and tragic war, to feel such existential angst was understandable. But in the 1950s, life would become steadily more prosperous and easy-going and art, including films, to some extent less adventurous. The early 1950s saw the birth of the consumer society (Magnusson 2002: 416). The economy continued to grow and be strong all the way through the 1950s and 1960s (until the oil crisis in the early 1970s). Reform also continued, now including three weeks' holiday (1951), the five-day, forty-hour working week and mandatory health insurance (1955). In 1951, the right to freedom of religion (and freedom *from* religion) was enshrined in the constitution. Before that one had to be a member of the Swedish church, unless one was of some other religious denomination.

With growing affluence and longer holidays, Swedes began to travel, and when the airline Scandinavian Airline System (SAS) was formed in 1951, followed by the opening of Arlanda airport just outside Stockholm, travelling abroad became much easier. Swedes also travelled around Europe by bus and went camping (Löfgren 2009). These changes affected Ekman and they were eventually incorporated in his films, as will be discussed in a later chapter.

In the 1960s, after having been in a coalition with the Farmers' Party (who had, in an effort to broaden their appeal, rebranded themselves as the Centre Party) for a while, the Social Democrats were once again alone in government. The prime minister, Tage Erlander, stated that the aim should now be to create 'the strong society' (Hadenius 2003: 132) and aim for even more equality. However, as the government spent more than it earned, something had to be done. Reluctant to raise taxes or to cut back on spending, they decided to bring back VAT (Hadenius 2003: 120). One thing this new money was needed for was to build more apartments and houses, since there was a shortage of both. On the whole, the general outlook was one of optimism and hope. The final conclusion of an investigation from 1955 sums it up: 'If we will have peace, the engineers promise us an almost new society in a couple of decades. The national economists at the same time calculate that in this new society the standard of living will be almost double what we have now' (quoted in Björck 2009: 348). This era was called Rekord-åren – the Record Years.

The 1960s were a time of great change, culturally, and also a time of social problems. Progress was made with regard to female emancipation. The number of women entering the workforce, both married and unmarried, increased dramatically, and the government's policy was one of equal pay for equal work (Dahlberg 1999: 204). This ties in with what can be called the feminist side of Ekman, and his recurring use of a strong, working woman as the central character. But he was ahead of the society in that respect. 'Increased equality' was the catchphrase of the 1960s and the 1970s (Magnusson 2002: 460), but, as will be argued, Ekman was already thinking along those lines from the early 1940s. However, even if there was increasing equality, in the late 1950s and 1960s drug abuse, crime and street fighting were also prevalent. For example, Sweden had more car thefts than any other country in Europe, comparative to the population, and youth gangs would battle with the police in the streets (Dahlberg 1999: 210).

Swedish design, both industrial and graphic, and art were in high demand, nationally as well as internationally, and in 1958 the Museum of Modern Art opened in Stockholm, with Pontus Hultén as its director. It quickly became one of the more important focal points of the global modern art circle, and brought a lot of North American art, such as that of Andy Warhol and Robert Rauschenberg, to Europe. Ekman incorporated some of these new ideas in art and design in his films in the late 1950s, both in production design and in cinematography.

Simultaneous with the rise of modern art and design, a big cultural shift took place in the living room of almost every household in Sweden. The television set arrived. It had been decided in Parliament that television should be free from commercials and that it should be an independent organisation, a public service inspired by the BBC, and work as a parallel institution to national radio (Hadenius 2003: 125). In 1957 there were thirty thousand television sets in Sweden; two years later there were five hundred thousand, among a population of 7.4 million. One of the reasons for this boom was the 1958 World Cup, which was held in Sweden and which saw Brazil beating Sweden in the final. This event is generally seen as the breakthrough of television in Sweden. The number of households with television sets went from two hundred thousand to two million in fewer than four years (Snickars 2008: 195).

Television brought about significant changes for the cinema, to audience behaviour and to ticket sales. Television also changed politics, family life, and design. Everybody would gather round the television, watching Swedish or foreign programmes. Among the most popular of the foreign television series was the American western series *Bonanza*, which was broadcast in Sweden from 1959 and led to a debate about violence on television and its effect on society (Alm 2009: 192), and later in the 1960s the British *Forsyte Saga* became a nation-wide success. The most popular Swedish television show was *Hylands hörna* (Hyland's Corner), which ran from 1962 to 1983 and was a Swedish version of *The Tonight Show Starring Johnny Carson* (1962–1992, USA). It was hosted by Lennart Hyland, who was already a well-established figure in Swedish society after a long career on the radio before he went into television. According to Furhammar, Hyland was 'for Sweden a completely unique phenomenon' (Furhammar 1991: 253, trans.) in his role as national father figure, comparable to the prime minster or the king perhaps. *Hylands hörna*'s aim was for Sweden to be like 'one big happy family' (Furhammar 1991: 253). It was here, in an unprecedented event, that the Swedish Prime Minister Tage Erlander appeared, in the first year of its broadcast, telling jokes and looking like an everyday person. This is an example of how television changed politics. It also changed how the home was furnished and designed, with the audience sitting at home on their 'TV-sofa', with their 'TV-flask' on the table. The television itself would be on the 'TV-shelf'. There was a whole range of products invented to cater to the new needs of the television-watching population. (It should also be mentioned that the Swedish furniture company IKEA opened its first store in 1958, making comparatively cheap and stylish furniture available to a large number of people.) As will be discussed later, in his films in the late 1950s and early 1960s Ekman often satirised television and the popular infatuation with it, along with other popular phenomena such as radio and the newly emerging trend of Continental coach travel.

CHAPTER 3
Swedish Cinema

There was a renaissance in Swedish cinema that really took off in 1940, in which
Ekman, as well as Bergman, played a vital part, but the cinema of the 1930s needs
to be discussed first to place the renaissance in a clearer light.

If the silent era was considered a 'golden age' of Swedish cinema, an expression commonly used about films made between 1913 and 1924 (cf. Cowie 1985;
Furhammar 1991; Bordwell & Thompson 2003), then the 1930s was widely
regarded as at best a nuisance, at worst a threat to society and morality. The
church thought that the cinema was 'immoral', thinking it was only about sexual
titillation; the army found it a disgrace due to the many comedies about silly soldiers; and the temperance movement found it appalling due to the excessive
consumption of alcohol portrayed (Furhammar 1991: 127–128) – there was even
a special genre called 'pilsnerfilm' ('beer movies'). The intelligentsia and leading
writers were particularly upset, led by the esteemed writer Vilhelm Moberg
(known internationally for his four books about Swedish immigrants in the USA,
beginning with *The Emigrants* (*Utvandrarna*, 1949)). It all came together in 1937
with a meeting at the Concert Hall in Stockholm, where Moberg and others made
their hostile feelings towards Swedish cinema perfectly clear. Moberg himself
said: 'We have been given the horrid gift of mass-reproduced infantilism and
stupidity' (quoted in Furhammar 1991: 128, trans.). According to Bordwell and
Thompson: 'Swedish cinema had been in eclipse since Victor Sjöström and
Mauritz Stiller were lured to Hollywood' (Bordwell & Thompson 2003: 383).

How did it come to this? Why did Swedish cinema go from being considered
a national treasure to something shameful? There were several reasons. In 1929
Swedish cinema was in a terrible state; in fact, not a single Swedish film premiered in the first half of 1929. This was the result of a perfect storm of financial
problems. The depression, mass unemployment and inflation, combined with
very strong competition from foreign films and the fact that Swedish production
companies had been reckless in their spending and were on the verge of bank-
ruptcy, all contributed to the near death of Swedish film production (Furhammar
1991: 91–93). But then came sound cinema, talking pictures, and that was the
beginning of a financial revival. The first Swedish films with sound were made in

1929. *Artificial Svensson* (*Konstgjorda Svensson*, Gustav Edgren, 1929) had a few sound effects and some dialogue. *The Dream Waltz* (*Säg det i toner*, Edvin Adolphson, Julius Jaenzon, 1929) had music and sound effects but no spoken dialogue. The first Swedish film with continuous dialogue was *When Roses Bloom* (*När rosorna slå ut*, Edvin Adolphson, 1930), although it was produced by the France-based company Paramount. *For Her Sake* (*För hennes skull*, Paul Merzbach, 1930) was the first film produced in Sweden with continuous dialogue (Natzén 2010: 117–119). Despite the novelty of hearing Swedish spoken on the screen, the new sound cinema did not generate any immediate box-office successes. Furhammar has argued that the box-office records for the early 1930s are very difficult to interpret, but that it appears that the depression made people less likely to go to the cinema (Furhammar 1991: 129–132), and it was not until 1933 that ticket sales started to increase. However, Swedish films became more popular and so more films were made. The production companies realised the value of using sound to appeal to the audience's sense of local pride. The films that were being made were vernacular and regional, and the production companies were finally making money again. So, after an uncertain start, including the economic depression and the suicide of the financier Ivar Kreuger in 1933, the Swedish film industry was back on its feet, although Gösta Werner argues that the output of the time was provincial and self-indulgent (Werner 1978: 65).

Considering that, globally, the late 1920s were among the best years world cinema had ever seen and that the 1930s were a great decade for French, American, British and Japanese cinema, it is even more disappointing that Swedish cinema was in such relatively bad shape. However, it is important to recall that the notion that the Swedish cinema of the 1930s was a complete failure is narrow-minded. In the 1930s between 250 and 300 Swedish films were made, which is more than twice as many as in the 1920s, and with so many films made, there were bound to be both good and bad releases. The 1930s were a period of rapid growth: the number of cinemas grew quickly and more than tripled during the decade (Furhammar 1991: 135) and according to Tytti Soila, 'virtually all domestic feature films produced were profitable' (Soila 1998: 173).

Criticism of Swedish films of the 1930s is not always fair. There were other works besides the 'immoral' films with no supposed artistic value that the critics railed against. One example is the work of the filmmaker Gustaf Molander, who might be called the grand old man of classical Swedish cinema. He wrote scripts for Victor Sjöström and Mauritz Stiller in the late 1910s and early 1920s and directed his first film, *The Tyranny of Hate* (*Bodakungen*), in 1920. During the 1930s he made a number of witty comedies and heartfelt melodramas, and among those is *Intermezzo* from 1936 starring Ingrid Bergman. In total he directed twenty-two films during the 1930s, an impressive number that also included the experimental *One Night* (*En natt*, 1931), which was influenced by Russian film-makers of the 1920s. Molander's films were even successful at international film festivals. *A Little Flirt* (*En stilla flirt*, 1934) won in Vienna in 1934, *Swedenhielms Family* (*Swedenhielms*, 1935) received an honorary mention in Venice in 1935 and *A Woman's Face* (*En kvinnas ansikte*, 1938) won an award for 'artistic perfection' in Venice in 1938. Molander, it should be added, was later to work with Ingmar Bergman, and Bengt Forslund has argued that Molander's interest and skill in telling women's stories mark him out as an important forerunner to Bergman (Forslund 2003: 91). Also relevant is that Ekman's father, Gösta Ekman, acted in several of Molander's films, including *Swedenhielms Family* and *Intermezzo*, where he played the father and Ekman played his son.

Another director worth mentioning is Schamyl Bauman. He has never been given much critical attention, but some, such as Per Olof Qvist, argue that Bauman can be seen as an important inspiration for Ingmar Bergman (Qvist 1995: 14). Towards the end of the 1930s Bauman had become an accomplished direc-tor, especially in directing actors, with a good ear for dialogue. Among the more prestigious films Bauman made were *Witches' Night* (*Häxnatten*, 1937), with Gösta Ekman, *Career* (*Karriär*, 1938), *The Two of Us* (*Vi två*, 1939) and *Wanted* (*Efterlyst*, 1939). Both *Career* and *The Two of Us* are reminiscent of films that Ekman would eventually make, and as Bauman and Ekman have many links Bauman will feature later in this book.

One filmmaker who was often political, in a Social Democratic consensus discourse, was Gustaf Edgren. Of the films he directed, most noteworthy here are *Karl Fredrik Reigns* and *The Red Day* (*Röda dagen*, 1931). The male star in these films was Sigurd Wallén, who also starred in two other films which had a strong Social Democratic profile, *With the People for the Motherland* (*Med folket för fos-terlandet*, 1938) and *Towards a New Dawn* (*Mot nya tider*, 1939). They were both films about the rise of a strong and just, Social Democratic Sweden. Besides play-ing the male lead, Wallén was also the director. Insofar as these films worked to establish a (mythical) image of Sweden, they easily lend themselves to studies from the perspective of national cinema, and the construction of an idea of the nation. In this they differ from the kind of films that were made in the 1940s, and Ekman's films in particular.

But even though Swedish films were available in abundance, foreign films were still much more popular, especially North American films. The greatest stars, after Greta Garbo, were Jeanette MacDonald and Maurice Chevalier (Furhammar 1991: 157). They acted together in six films from 1929 to 1934, five of which were directed by Ernst Lubitsch, either alone or together with George Cukor. It can probably be taken for granted that Hasse Ekman saw these films, and that these years were very formative for him as a filmmaker. It is an important factor in Ekman's career that his sources of inspiration were international, such as Lubitsch and Jean Renoir, rather than Swedish. That influence began in the 1930s. After the MacDonald/Chevalier films, Lubitsch made films such as *Design for Living* (1933) and *The Shop Around the Corner* (1940). The French filmmaker Marcel Carné, who will be discussed in a later chapter, also made several impor-tant films during the decade such as *Hôtel du Nord* (1938) and *Port of Shadows* (*Quai de brumes*, 1938). Renoir made films such as *Boudu Saved from Drowning* (*Boudu sauvé des eaux*, 1932), *The Crime of Monsieur Lange* (*Le crime de M. Lange*, 1935), *La Grande Illusion* (1937) and *The Rules of the Game* (*La règle du jeu*, 1939).

So, to conclude, the audience in the 1930s had many films to choose from, both domestic and foreign, both quality and mundane. With regard to the more mundane Swedish films that were produced, Furhammar sums them up thus: 'It was quite simply a picture of the Swedish *folkhem*' (Furhammar 1991: 161, trans.). Then came the Second World War and everything changed.

These were sensitive times and the political situation was tense. There was much state censorship and it is reasonable to assume that this also led to a kind of self-censorship. Sweden's official policy during the war was neutrality, so films arguing for one side over the other were rarely released. Foreign films were also being censored or forbidden. This mostly affected films from the Allies, particu-larly the US. But, as Soila points out: 'there was one category that was consis-tently allowed through and that was the Finnish, frequently avidly anti-Russian, films that were imported into the country' (Soila 1998: 179). This was because Sweden's official policy in the war between Finland and the Soviet Union was not neutral but non-combative. Although politically sensitive, nevertheless, from an economic viewpoint, the war years were a glorious time for the Swedish film industry. Due to the war it was hard for foreign films to come to Swedish cinemas, not least French films, so there was less competition from abroad. At the same time, the public was going to the cinema like never before. Despite the fact that the cinemas were cold during winter due to rationing, audiences almost doubled, from thirteen million to twenty-three million visitors a year in Stockholm and Göteborg between 1936 and 1945 (Furhammar 1991: 170). The authorities responded to this huge increase in box-office receipts with a change in the tax code, so there was a kind of film tax which became mandatory in 1940.

As there was a war on and times were precarious, not all output could be described as quality productions. Many films were made to foster patriotism and love of the countryside. These films were often short, and made not only by the film studios but sometimes by the SIS (the State Board of Information) or even by the military. Usually they depicted Swedish history or Swedish nature, but according to Furhammar, they were decidedly 'non-military' and 'free of aggression' (Furhammar 1991: 168, trans.). A number of feature films were also made for similar purposes, and these films could be about the military, but in accordance with Sweden's neutrality, the films did not specify who was fighting whom, or where – although, again, this did not prevent films from being made that were specifically about the war in Finland. Ekman made one such film, *A Day Will Come* (*En dag skall gry*, 1944).

During the 1930s the studio system had been very strong in Sweden and in some ways it continued to be so in the 1940s. The biggest studio was still SF, together with Europa Film and the up-and-coming Sandrew. As in Hollywood, the studios had their contracted writers, directors, actors and technicians. Films had to be made on budget and on time. Hasse Ekman once quipped that on an ordinary day in the studio, he would be making a film in one corner, Arne Mattsson would be making a film in another corner, Alf Sjöberg in a third corner and in the fourth corner carpenters would be building a new set (cited in Åhlund & Carlsson 1993). The big studios were also vertically integrated, meaning that they controlled the production, distribution and exhibition of all their films. At the same time the owner structure was complicated due to dealings between the studios, in that they bought and sold parts of each other back and forth (Furhammar 1991: 174).

The various studios had their differences, however. Some were interested in comedies, some were more interested in highbrow dramas, and some focused on more lowbrow farces. But there was at the same time a general wish to make more complex films with a message, and one way in which this became apparent was with the hiring of new heads of production at both SF and Sandrew. At SF, Carl-Anders Dymling, a man with a cultural outlook, took over in 1942, and he in turn hired Victor Sjöström as artistic adviser. Dymling even wrote editorials in film journals where he, among other things, advocated the importance of high-quality productions. At Sandrew, a leading film critic and film historian, Rune Waldekranz, was made head of production. His vision was to get the best filmmakers and give them money and a free hand and in so doing create a genuine art cinema. Another important film company was Terra, headed by Lorens Marmstedt. It was at Terra that Hasse Ekman would make his first films, and Terra was at the time considered to be a high-quality studio. This is emphasised by the fact that as part of Sandrew's aim to further its artistic ambitions, it aligned itself with Terra and Marmstedt (Furhammar 1991: 178).

Comedies and films dealing with social issues were common, as were adaptations of Swedish literary classics. Statistically, a major change occurred towards the end of the Second World War. Whereas during the 1930s and early 1940s comedies were the most common kind of films, from 1943 a large number of dramatic films were also produced, while roughly the same number of comedies were being made. Many of the dramatic films that were being produced were made by new filmmakers. So this new focus was partly due to a new generation of filmmakers appearing. (That more dramatic films were made is in itself of course not a proof of quality; it is only a proof of change.) But, as Soila argues, 'the sizeable repertory makes it difficult to determine clear thematic lines in the wartime production of films, because virtually all genres, ideas and patterns were tested' (Soila 1998: 181). Furhammar argues that it became more common to discuss religious matters in films, something which had been almost non-existent as a theme in the 1930s (Furhammar 1991: 192), and Werner argues that the filmmakers became more courageous and achieved a considerably higher level of stylistic awareness (Werner 1978: 82). Furhammar even argues that it was specifically the visual aspects of Swedish cinema in the 1940s that constituted the real artistic advance (Furhammar 1991: 193–194). But there were changes when it came to scriptwriting as well. In Sweden during the 1920s, Stiller, Sjöström and Georg af Klercker often wrote their own screenplays, together with Gustaf Molander, but in the 1930s this was most unusual. This changed with the newer generation of filmmakers who were writer-directors. Although it was not the first time that one individual was both a writer and a director, it was now the first time this became common, even a standard. Ekman was such a filmmaker.

It has been claimed that 1940 is something of a watershed in Swedish cinema history and that this is owing to one film, *A Crime (Ett brott)*, directed by Anders

Henriksson. The critics at the time certainly talked about it in such terms. Yet such a position can be contested. If 1940 is at all to be considered a watershed, it is not just because of *A Crime*, but rather because of a number of releases that clearly indicated that a new approach to filmmaking was becoming widespread. Other films released the same year worth mentioning are Alf Sjöberg's *They Staked Their Lives* (*Med livet som insats*), Åke Ohberg's *Romance* (*Romans*) and Per Lindberg's *Steel* (*Stål*), a film about the industrial town of Falun. Another important film of 1940 was *With You in My Arms*, Ekman's first film as writer and director, less for its intrinsic qualities than for its very appearance, or rather the appearance of Ekman. As will be elaborated upon in the next chapter, it was considered to be a breath of fresh air in Swedish cinema and its immediate success led the way to Ekman's further career.

Among the directors working during the war years, Alf Sjöberg stands out. According to Peter Cowie: 'Next to Bergman ... Sjöberg must be accounted the most significant Swedish director of that long, uneven period stretching from the departure of Sjöström and Stiller for Hollywood in the mid-1920s and the establishment of the Swedish Film Institute in 1963' (Cowie 1985: 50). Whilst that is a questionable statement there is no question regarding Sjöberg's importance and high standing in Swedish cinema of this period. Sjöberg's most famous film is probably *Torment* aka *Frenzy* (*Hets*, 1944) but it is admittedly more famous for being written by Ingmar Bergman, his first credited screenplay, than for being directed by Sjöberg. Among Sjöberg's most interesting films are *Home from Babylon* (*Hem från Babylon*, 1941), *The Heavenly Play* (*Himlaspelet*, 1942) and *Only a Mother* (*Bara en mor*, 1949). His artistically most accomplished film, however, was *Miss Julie* (*Fröken Julie*, 1951), adapted from August Strindberg's play, which Sjöberg had already directed on the stage. It was shot by a distant relative of Strindberg, Göran Strindberg, who was one of Sweden's leading cinematographers at this point. On stage Sjöberg had been working with time and space in an unusual way, letting scenes set in the past and scenes set in the present play beside each other simultaneously, and he brought this approach with him to the film, making *Miss Julie* a bold experiment in both the use of depth of field and narrative structure. It was a critical success, at home and abroad, winning numerous awards in South America and the Grand Prix at Cannes (sharing it with *Miracle in Milan* (*Miracolo a Milano*, Vittorio de Sica, 1951)). Sjöberg can be seen as a major influence on Bergman, but to a lesser degree on Ekman. Of greater personal importance for Ekman was Schamyl Bauman, although Bauman had lost the intimate touch that he had in the 1930s. He was now making mostly routine comedies. However, they were very profitable and Bauman still sometimes managed to return to his sense of everyday realism.

Other names that must be mentioned are Erik 'Hampe' Faustman, Per Lindberg, Olof Molander, Arne Mattsson and, of course, the ubiquitous Gustaf Molander. Of all major Swedish directors, Erik 'Hampe' Faustman was the most overtly political, with a strong socialist bent. His first film was *Night in Harbour* (*Natt i hamn*, 1943), a film about seamen and saboteurs at the height of the Second World War. As a studio director, he had to make films that were not necessarily of his choosing, and it was not until the late 1940s that he really found his niche with angry films about the working class such as *When the Meadows Are in Bloom* (*När ängarna blomma*, 1946), *Lars Hård* (1948), *Foreign Harbour* (*Främmande hamn*, 1948) and *Vagabond Blacksmiths* (*Smeder på luffen*, 1949). *When the Meadows Are in Bloom* is a harsh look at the life of *statarna*, peasants living in almost slave-like conditions; *Lars Hård* tells the story of a man whose parents were *statare* and who is sent to prison for manslaughter; and *Foreign Harbour* is about Swedish dock workers in the Polish harbour town of Gdynia who strike to prevent a ship bound for the fascists in Spain leaving the harbour. *Vagabond Blacksmiths* is the story of three blacksmiths who leave town and set out on a walk through the country, going from job to job, and experiencing oppression from the capitalists and the authorities and solidarity and camaraderie among the workers.

Per Lindberg made only a handful of films. He was, like Sjöberg, a man of the theatre. The few films he made were rather experimental and offbeat. Again, like Sjöberg, Lindberg made films in the 1920s, including two in 1923, but then left filmmaking until the war years, making seven films between 1939 and 1941. After that he stopped, possibly due to the fact that his experiments were not widely appreciated (Werner 1978: 83–85). But one of them, *Rejoice While You're Young, Fellow Cadets* (*Gläd dig i din ungdom*, 1939), did win an award at the Venice Biennale. Olof Molander (brother of Gustaf) also made just a handful of films, and in them he experimented with narrative and visuals. The films often have a loose structure with an associative montage, disrupting both time and space, and telling their stories in a non-linear way. The visual style is expressionistic, with stark contrasts between light and darkness, and elaborate use of perspectives and depth. Among his six films from the 1940s, *Imprisoned Women* (*Kvinnor i fångenskap*, 1943) and *Appassionata* (1944) are particularly noteworthy.

Arne Mattsson made his first film in 1944, ...*And All These Women* (... *och alla dessa kvinnor*), which was not a success, but Mattsson was noted for his visual sense. He continued to work hard over the following years, with his fourth film, *Sussie* (1945), being regarded by the critics at the time as his artistic breakthrough. However, Mattsson, who soon developed an interest in psychology and thrillers, or perhaps psychological thrillers, was not to become a really big name until the 1950s when he made *One Summer of Happiness* (*Hon dansade en sommar*, 1951), and followed it with such works as the war drama *The Bread of Love* (*Kärlekens bröd*, 1953) and *Salka Valka* (1954), based on a novel by the Icelandic Nobel Prize-winner Halldor Laxness. Mattsson was above all else a visual filmmaker, using the camera and the mise-en-scène to create striking and symbolic compositions, with elaborate camera movements and expressive lightning. Then there was Arne Sucksdorff, an experimental documentary filmmaker. He made several short films in the 1940s which were incredibly well edited. Like many of the above-mentioned filmmakers, he had an expressionistic visual style. His films, some made in Sweden and some in India, won him awards all over the world and one of them, *Symphony of a City* (*Människor i stad*, 1947), was the first Swedish film to win an Academy Award.

So during the war years there was a sudden explosion of rich, nuanced and thought-provoking films, many visual and narrative experiments and the rise of a new generation of filmmakers, who sometimes worked with each other. In addition, a few filmmakers (Sjöberg, Lindberg, Olof Molander) who had not been making films for a decade or so returned with new releases. All of these things, combined with a large audience interested in watching Swedish films and new producers interested in producing high-quality films, justify calling this time a renaissance for Swedish cinema and Ekman was both a part of this and a result of this new era. Considering that this era included a number of debutant filmmakers, working together and making films that constituted a clear break from what came before, it is possible to call it a Swedish New Wave – at least, in an interview from 1962 Ingmar Bergman said that during the 1940s it felt like being part of a new wave (Kindblom 2006: 94). For Sweden, this wave lasted for about a decade, because in the immediate post-war years things continued to be good for filmmakers. It is tempting to compare Sweden with the UK during the 1940s, as that country also had something of a cinematic renaissance at that time. It seems as if the constant threat of war, combined with the fact that there never was an enemy invasion, led to an unusually vibrant cinema. With artists wanting to deal with social anxieties in radical ways, and with the population at large eager both to escape from, and engage with, the existential crisis that the war can be said to have brought on, these were good years for films and filmmaking. The fact that neither Sweden nor the UK was invaded meant that production never came to an end and was never shut down, and that the countries could remain free and democratic. This set the two countries apart from most other countries in Europe in the 1940s.

The post-war years were years of paradox for the Swedish film industry. On the one hand, there were many economic problems, but on the other, the quality and international prestige of many of the films being made were almost unparalleled in Swedish film history. The economic difficulties were partly due to the fact that the cost of running the cinemas was increasing more than the price of the tickets was (Furhammar 1991: 205). There was also a substantial drop in the number of people who went to see Swedish films, even though the number of films made each year was the same as during the war years – around forty per year. (ibid.: 199). It was not that the audience had stopped going to the cinema in general; they were just as eager as before, but they were not as interested in Swedish films any more. In fact, the producers were at a loss to determine exactly what kind of domestic films the audience wanted (ibid.: 199). What mostly appealed to the audience were British, French and Italian films. On top of this, in 1948 the government decided to substantially increase what was called an 'entertainment tax', which increased the price of a ticket (ibid.: 205). But the increase went to the Ministry of Finance, not to the cinema owners. The cost of raw film stock also rose, while the krona was devalued (Soila 1998: 194). Several production companies were either bought by bigger players or went bankrupt in the post-war era. The biggest company, SF, was cautious, not to say conservative, but still it had box-office failures.

And yet these were good years for filmmakers, and a lot of new ground was covered. The first Swedish film in colour was made in 1946, somewhat late from an international perspective, and there were experiments with narrative, form and themes. A booming international festival circuit rewarded many of these films, beginning with *Torment* winning the Cannes Grand Prix in 1946 (the Grand Prix would be called the Palme d'Or from 1955). This international prestige was matched at home by the fact that both audiences and media had begun to take cinema more seriously. Film journals devoted to serious criticism were launched; cooperative or communal film clubs were started. A new kind of audience emerged, which Furhammar calls 'an elite audience' (Furhammar 1991: 202, trans.) and Soila calls 'the connoisseurs' (Soila 1998: 197). This audience wanted to see intelligent, challenging and sophisticated films.

According to Soila, there had not been a large variety of genres in Swedish cinemas. The films were either melodramas or farcical comedies, and this was due to Sweden being a small market in which the films had to please as many as possible (Soila 1998: 195–196). But this was now beginning to change as well. One very prominent genre was what might be called the 'peasantry drama'. As already mentioned, this was a time of rapid urbanisation; the shift from rural to urban areas, amid an overall shift from farming to industrialisation, caused much anxiety and these films reflect that. They usually fall into three different types: a serious and tragic drama, often in a historical setting; a farcical comedy; or a melancholy drama about the inevitability of change. This was apparently exactly what the audience wanted. A film of the first type was *Sunshine Follows Rain* (*Driver dagg, faller regn*, Gustaf Edgren, 1946), which was SF's biggest box-office success since the company had been founded. A film of the second type was the *Åsa-Nisse* series, most of them produced by AB Svensk Talfilm, which drew millions of cinemagoers to each film. The prime example of the third kind was Arne Mattsson's phenomenally successful *One Summer of Happiness*. Per Olov Qvist adds an additional subgenre to the rural films: the archipelago film (Qvist 1986). According to Soila: 'The dichotomy of country–city has always been a feature of Swedish film but this new nostalgic dimension came about through an awareness of the obsolescence of rural life' (Soila 1998: 191). Furhammar has argued, however, that many films made during this period showed a genuine, and increasing, willingness to engage with society and to discuss important issues, and that the most common theme is the conflict between the individual and the collective (Furhammar 1991: 229). This can also be seen as the conflict between the collective, communal life in the rural areas and the more individualistic and anonymous life in the big city. It is important to mention this because Hasse Ekman did not make films with rural settings and themes. It is rather the case that his unusual urbanity is something which sets him apart from other filmmakers, and this will be discussed later in the book.

So filmmakers were pushing the boundaries and could still make challenging and personal films. With the production companies often in disarray, it became easier for filmmakers to work without interference and to be able to move around among the studios, feeling less committed to any of them. It should be emphasised that, usually, the director wrote the script alone or sometimes in collaboration, and that this is the case in almost all of the films mentioned in this chapter. The skills and technical mastery already alluded to were just as apparent in the post-war area. What changed was that a new generation of actors appeared and, unlike in earlier years, the actors were no longer playing a particular 'type', but were being used by the directors to create real characters (Furhammar 1991: 222). In this respect, Ekman was of considerable importance.

The end of censorship and increasing social liberalisation in Sweden also affected the films being made. Films and filmmakers became more outspoken, socially as well as politically. They still worked within the general confines of the studio context but in such a rich and experimental context the films made were not necessarily routine and formulaic. Ekman, while being a part of the 'system', was also in many ways his own man. (The balance between individuality and context will be explored in later chapters.)

The early 1950s were still dynamic and dramatic. There were bigger audiences than ever before and there were a large number of quality films being made, including some of Ekman's best. There was also among critics and intellectuals a strong, and increasing, interest in cinema as an art form, even though television was to become the dominant source of popular entertainment. These were years when Swedish cinema regained the worldwide reputation it had enjoyed in the early 1920s. In 1951, besides the festival successes of *Miss Julie*, *Living on 'Hope'* (*Leva på 'Hoppet'*, Göran Gentele, 1951) won the Silver Bear at the Berlin Film Festival, the Swedish/Norwegian co-production *Kon-tiki* (Thor Heyerdahl, 1950) won an Academy Award for best documentary and *While the City Sleeps* (*Medan staden sover*, Lars-Eric Kjellgren, 1950) won the Silver Laurel Award in Hollywood. The next year, 1952, saw *One Summer of Happiness* win the Golden Bear at Berlin and *An Indian Village* (*Indisk by*, Arne Sucksdorff, 1951) win the Prix Spécial du Jury at Cannes. In 1953, *Sawdust and Tinsel* (*Gycklarnas afton*, Ingmar Bergman, 1953), symptomatic of the producer Rune Waldekranz's drive for high-quality films, won the Grand Prize at the São Paulo Film Festival.

Since 1940 Swedish cinema had been rich and vibrant, experimental and profitable. But things began to change in the early 1950s. The film studios were nervous, and the situation was fragile. At the end of the 1940s the studios were restive over the government's film policy, especially the doubling of tax on ticket sales, and starting on 1 January 1951 all film production was shut down in what was called '*filmstoppet*'. During this protest, a sort of strike, no studio films were made except Arne Mattsson's *One Summer of Happiness*, which for some reason received a free pass by the film producers' organisation. After six months the government caved in and agreed that the film producers needed state funding for support (Soila 1998: 195), and this addressed the difficulties arising from the previously increased 'entertainment tax'. But during the 1950s filmmakers found it more and more difficult to make challenging films and with society becoming more affluent and content, there was arguably less of a market for, and perhaps less urgency on the part of filmmakers to make, films with deeper, existential themes. And this affected Ekman too. If the 1940s had been a renaissance, around 1953 that era came to an end with Bergman's *Sawdust and Tinsel*, Ekman's *Gabrielle* (1954) and Sucksdorff's first full-length documentary, *The Great Adventure* (*Det stora äventyret*, 1953). Although there was still challenging work made, the late 1950s saw primarily detective stories and adaptations of Astrid Lindgren's novels, several of which became fine films. Financially, things would soon get much worse, because now television appeared.

If there is one word that best sums up this period in Swedish cinema it is 'crisis'. In 1956, 78.2 million tickets were sold in Sweden, generating 180 million kronor. In 1960, 55 million tickets were sold, generating 120 million kronor. In 1961, 40 million tickets were sold, and in 1972, only 22.5 million. Such a drastic decline did of course have a major impact on almost all aspects of film production. At first the film industry was in a state of denial as to the reasons for this, and the decline in sales was blamed on the influenza epidemic, or on the popular taste for joyriding, or on other implausible factors. However, as Furhammar writes, '[n]othing could eventually hide the obvious fact that TV was the concrete and sufficient reason' for this decline and for the 'state of catastrophic crisis' (Furhammar 1991: 249, trans.). In 1957 an investigation was undertaken into the state of the cinema in Sweden and the results were presented in 1959. The report found that Sweden had, relative to its population size, more cinemas than almost any other country in the world, but that the attendance rate was among the lowest in the world (Furhammar 1991: 262). The government implemented a new tax regime, with various tax cuts, tax breaks and tax refunds. In 1959, of the money the state received from ticket sales for black-and-white films, 30 per cent was refunded while for colour films, 45 per cent was refunded. But the crisis intensified and in 1962 Harry Schein, a leading film critic at *Bonniers Litterära Magasin* (*BLM*) and friend of both Bergman and leading members of the Social Democratic Party, suggested a complete overhaul of the system. This resulted in the creation of the Swedish Film Institute in 1963, with Schein as its director.

It is ironic that techniques that in many countries were used by the film producers as weapons to counter the allure of television, namely colour and widescreen, in Sweden now saw something of a backlash. For one thing, it was more expensive to shoot in these formats than in the older ones. Secondly, since television was at the time available only as a monochrome medium, the television channels would not buy films shot in colour. This made it an even worse investment for the producers to shoot in colour at the time. These factors meant that the production of colour films and widescreen films actually declined in the late 1950s (ibid.: 259). During such a calamitous time the scope for being adventurous as a filmmaker was very limited. Fewer films were made in general, and they were primarily in mainstream genres: thrillers or comedies.

Among the more prestigious filmmakers, Bergman stood out. He was generally considered by the critics as being the cinema's leading auteur. Scarcely anybody else was even trying to be as artistically daring and challenging. In 1962 the magazine *Folket i bild* cancelled its annual award for distinguished achievements in Swedish cinema since there was only one contender: Bergman (ibid.: 271). Bergman was working under contract at SF, one of the few studios which was fully functioning, and he had the trust of Carl-Anders Dymling, the head of the studio. After the international successes of *Smiles of a Summer Night* (*Sommarnattens leende*, 1955), including winning the prize for best film at Cannes, Bergman was given more or less a free hand. By making one or two films a year, Bergman continued to develop as a filmmaker. Ekman was now also contracted with SF so both worked under Dymling. (This relationship and competition between Ekman and Bergman will be analysed later.) Bergman's importance increased when Dymling died in 1961 and was replaced by Kenne Fant, as Fant made Bergman his close adviser.

Of the older generation of filmmakers most had disappeared. Hampe Faustman died in 1961, Arne Sucksdorff made two feature-length financial disasters and moved to Brazil in the early 1960s, and Schamyl Bauman retired in 1958. Gustaf Molander made his penultimate film in 1956, only returning to the cinema in 1967 to make a short film, as part of *Stimulantia*, an anthology film with nine different directors, including Bergman. Alf Sjöberg made a few films, but struggled as he was not popular with the critics or the public, so he mainly worked in the theatre. Arne Mattsson was still prolific and successful, with a series of visually bold thrillers. However, as Furhammar argues: 'it is saddening in hindsight to see how many filmmakers ... experienced artistic decline during the decade following the end of the Second World War' (ibid.: 232, trans.).

The most important films at the beginning of the 1960s were of a different kind. A new tradition of Swedish filmmakers appeared, such as Bo Widerberg, Mai Zetterling, Jörn Donner, Jan Troell and Vilgot Sjöman. It would be a mistake to call this a new generation, or a young generation. They were all older than thirty, and some were only a few years younger than Bergman and Ekman. But they were more politically engaged, and these were filmmakers who were influenced by the French New Wave. Like the French, some of them were also critics and writers and they were justifiably critical of the conservative and stale Swedish film climate of the late 1950s. Widerberg had in 1962 written a series of articles about the state of Swedish cinema which were published together under the name *Visionen i svensk film* (The Vision in Swedish Cinema). There, Widerberg attacked the production companies for not allowing filmmakers to make personal and meaningful films, and criticised Bergman for not making films that were about the everyday problems of the common man. Widerberg is quoted by Cowie as saying: 'Every new Swedish film was a disaster, it had absolutely no connection with modern society' (Cowie 1985: 65). Soon Widerberg and his friends would be making socially engaged films and these filmmakers and their films not only altered the cinematic landscape but also changed audiences' and critics' perceptions of what a film could and should look like. The established filmmakers struggled with this. Bergman was the only one of them who successfully managed to negotiate this new landscape, even though he was often criticised by the newcomers for not being political enough. It was in this rapidly changing context that Ekman bid farewell to filmmaking.

CHAPTER 4
Hasse Ekman in the Renaissance

During the 1920s and 1930s one of the greatest stars of the Swedish stage was Gösta Ekman. He also acted in films, both in the silent era and well into the 1930s, in Sweden as well as abroad. His son, Hasse, was born in 1915 in Stockholm, and from the start he was involved in the world of the theatre and show business. At the age of eight Hasse acted, together with his father, in the film *The Young Nobleman* (*Unga greven tar flickan och priset*, Rune Carlsten, 1924). Living in such a world of acting and actors inevitably affected young Ekman. Around the time of the making of *The Young Nobleman*, he said to a friend: 'It's spooky actually. Sometimes I feel like the world is just one big theatre, and that every human being is playing a part. Some are good at it, some are bad. But we never get to read any reviews. Are you always yourself? ... I'm not, but that might not be unusual for a theatre child' (Ekman 1933: 216, trans.). That this was important for Ekman is perhaps indicated by the fact that he quoted it again in his second autobiography, *Den vackra ankungen* (Ekman 1955: 240). It is interesting that already as a boy he was thinking about something that would be a major theme in his body of work: role-playing.

In the early 1930s Ekman did odd jobs in the theatre and in film. In 1934 he got his first chance to direct for the stage, together with Per Lindberg. The play was Tolstoy's *The Man Who Was Dead*. In 1935 Ekman joined a film magazine called *Filmbilden* (*The Film Image*; for an analysis of this magazine see Habel (2002)) and soon thereafter he went to Hollywood to do research. He was there for almost seven months and with his background and journalistic credentials he was able to meet many important people, such as the directors Frank Capra and George Cukor (Forslund 1982: 138–139). This trip would be significant for Ekman as it enabled him to learn the craft of filmmaking by talking to professionals, seeing them on the set, and watching a lot of films. The year after the trip to Hollywood Ekman had his breakthrough as an actor, in Gustaf Molander's *Intermezzo*, where he was again acting with his father. Gösta Ekman plays a world-famous violinist who is travelling all over Sweden and Europe doing concerts, whilst his long-suffering wife and two children are left at home. The son is played by Hasse Ekman. Towards the end of the film there is a scene in which the son is accusing the father of abandoning them, saying that he does not care for them any longer. The conflict between a son and his father, or a father figure, would be a recurring theme in Ekman's own films.

Ekman also worked on film scripts and in 1938 for the first time one of his scripts was turned into a film. It was called *Thunder and Lightning* (*Blixt och dunder*, Anders Henriksson); Ekman based the script on a story by P.G. Wodehouse called *Summer Lightning*. The book had been published in Swedish in 1935, and Wodehouse would remain one of Ekman's key influences. The film received moderately good reviews and Ekman was congratulated for his adaptation. But it would still be two years until Ekman could direct his own script.

In the first scene of *With You in My Arms*, Ekman's first film as writer and director, a well-dressed man is walking down a street. He approaches a boy selling newspapers and says, in English, 'Good morning, my good man. Nice weather today'. The boy looks puzzled and the well-dressed man says, now in Swedish, 'Oh, forgive me; I thought I was in London'. After having bought a newspaper, the man then proceeds to an apartment where he walks in, and it becomes apparent that he works there as a butler or manservant. He goes around, tidying things up (apparently the person who lives in the apartment has had some kind of party), whilst looking for his employer, whom he refers to as '*Direktören*' (managing director). He enters the bedroom where someone is sleeping, completely covered by the blanket. When the butler shakes the sleeping person he is startled to find that it is not Direktören but a cab driver. After some confusion it appears that the cab driver had followed Direktören up the stairs the previous night. Now he is sleeping in the bed and Direktören is sleeping in the bathtub. This is a typical farcical opening of a comedy of mixed up identities set among the upper classes, those who have the time and money to sleep in on a weekday and employ a butler. Even though this was an original script by Ekman, he was still writing as if under the influence of Wodehouse. But at the same time he had already begun developing his own ideas.

What happens next is that this Direktören, whose name is Krister Dahl, goes for a game of golf. Whilst playing, he is hit on the head by a golf ball and loses his memory. He no longer knows who he is; not even his name. He finds a wallet and, thinking it is his, he now believes he is that person whose name is in the wallet. Eventually he finds out that this is a mistake and he is somebody else. This is a relief to him since he did not like the person he thought he was. The problem is that by this time he has fallen in love. The person he has fallen in love with is the woman he was once married to and whom he now has happened to meet by chance.

When he eventually learns who he is, he also learns that the person he is, Krister Dahl, was not a very nice person: lazy, unreliable, spoilt and a womaniser. (As his butler says, he was a: 'typical product of the upper class, with all the vices and charms of the upper class'.). Now Dahl sets out to do good, by sorting out his affairs and making up with his ex-wife. But when he says that from now on he is going to be a responsible citizen the response from her is: 'Oh, really? That sounds boring'.

On the surface it is a typical Swedish story, which is seemingly arguing, in Soila's words, that 'wealth is not always a precondition of happiness, but that hard work, honesty and contentedness are' (Soila 1998: 176). It is also about the mixing of the classes in a manner consonant with *folkhemmet*, the 'people's society' and the spirit of Saltsjöbaden – in other words, a sense of natural bonds between people who might not be equals but are treated as such. But at the same time there is an English feeling to the film and the Wodehousian elements are noticeable. There are also a few things that set it apart from Swedish cinema of the time. It is too early to speak of a particular Ekman style, but a few touches predict things to come. According to Furhammar, this film was: 'a playful challenge, a youthful witty provocation with a touch of international modernity right in the heart of the stale Swedish cinema of the 1930s' (Furhammar 1993: 42, trans.). In what way?

The most obvious way is through the freewheeling improvisations. In one scene all the leading characters suddenly burst out singing an opera, in a parody of Verdi. There is an element of crazy comedy here, a sense of anarchy waiting to break out, which was something Ekman would come back to in his later years, especially in his theatre work. But perhaps the most important elements for Furhammar are the leading man and the leading lady. They are played by Edvin Adolphson and Karin Ekelund, who had earlier that year played the lead characters in the previously mentioned *A Crime*. It was a serious drama, nothing at all like a crazy comedy. For Furhammar, Ekman was here deliberately turning things around by making this grave couple suddenly playful and mischievous. It should, however, be pointed out that it was not the first time either Ekelund or Adolphson played comedy and most of Ekelund's career so far had been in comic roles. The particular scenes, described above, are more relevant for arguing for Ekman as an auteur.

The reason for describing the opening scene in such detail is to exemplify the way in which many of Ekman's films are not geographically grounded: they could be set anywhere, apparently almost to the point that the characters themselves are a bit lost as to where they are. This is accompanied by the wish to be somewhere else. If the butler did think he was in London, then maybe that was because that is where he really wanted to be.

The key aspect of the second scene described above is the use of the word 'boring' (or 'dull'). It would not be worth mentioning were it only in reference to this one film, but the argument that one must not be dull is a recurring theme in Ekman's films. It can be argued that this is a way for Ekman to distance himself from the Swedish model of scientific solutions, hard work and character building. The world as it is presented in Ekman's films can feel like a straitjacket in which the worst outcome is to be caught up in the ennui of bourgeois living. This was clearly developed in Ekman's later films.

As Furhammar argues, it is interesting that, already in this first film, Ekman takes up the subject of identity and its fluidity (Furhammar 1993: 40). It is a story about the search for self, albeit made in a whimsical manner. This is another common theme in Ekman's films: the looseness and fluidity of identities, and how they can be a mask to hide behind. Also present is a talent for showing something symbolically, instead of explicitly showing what is happening. This can be used either to heighten the emotional impact or to suggest erotic feelings or events (such as adultery). One example of this from With You in My Arms takes place in a bedroom where Krister Dahl's ex-wife and new lover, Barbro, is seen sleeping in her bed. She wakes up with a big smile on her face, looking very content, and she reaches out to the side of the bed where her partner would be sleeping, patting it. Then she looks puzzled because there is nobody there. When the maid comes in she says: 'I had such a beautiful dream'. The implication, which is further underlined by visual means, is that in her dream she had sex, and she woke up at the point of having an orgasm.

When With You in My Arms was released the critics were favourably impressed. One reviewer from the leading daily Stockholms-Tidningen wrote: 'The young P.G. Wodehouse expert and modern film expert Hasse Ekman has got fresh input from screwball comedies. But the playful, continentally smooth and elegant tone of his first film [is] un-Swedish in that it is chemically unsentimental' (Larz 1940, trans.). Here, Ekman's work is compared to Hollywood cinema, especially the work of Garson Kanin.[1] So the critics felt that the film was a breath of fresh air, and it is easy to see why.

With You in My Arms was not the only film Ekman was involved with in 1940. He and Schamyl Bauman also made three films together: *Heroes in Yellow and Blue* (*Hjältar i gult och blått*), *A Man in Full* (*Karl för sin hatt*) and *Swing It, Teacher!* ('*Swing it' magistern!*). Bauman directed and he and Ekman wrote the scripts together, and this collaboration with Bauman was very important for Ekman's career. At least one of the films, *Swing It, Teacher!*, has become a Swedish classic, but all three of them were at the time considered by critics to be something new and fresh. The same point they had made about *With You in My Arms* was made about these films. They were different from early Swedish films – more modern, and it was the scripts that the critics felt made such a difference. The story of *Swing It, Teacher!* is about the conflict brought about when a young girl tries to introduce jazz at her old-fashioned school. There is a parallel there to Ekman's efforts to bring a new, more modern approach to filmmaking, inspired by Hollywood and French cinema. Unlike the girl in the film, however, he was met with instant and almost unified approval.

So Ekman was off to a good start. For his next film, he would do something different. In keeping with the mood of the time, he made a film about the military, *The First Division* (*Första divisionen*, 1941). Alvar Zacke, a journalist from Stockholm with a special interest in flying, came up with the idea and wrote the script together with Ekman. In the first scene a young sub-lieutenant[2] in the Swedish air force arrives at a train station in the north of Sweden. He is met by an old friend and they walk together to the base. The scene with the two of them walking is shot in one take, with the camera in front of them, tracking backwards. After many adventures and intrigues at the base, the sub-lieutenant, who is played by Ekman, dies in a plane crash (this is not a war film and all the flying is for practice only). The last scene of the film takes place at the same train station, where another young sub-lieutenant arrives to take the place of the first. This is the first example of what would become something of a trademark for Ekman, the way he often ends a film with a scene that is a repetition of the opening scene, albeit with a slight but important difference. The long take that opens the film would also become something of a trademark of Ekman's style.

With You in My Arms was received favourably by the critics, and *The First Division* received even better reviews. The most noteworthy comment is perhaps from the leading Swedish daily *Dagens Nyheter*: 'Has there ever since the dawn of sound pictures been a film in this country which is in every sense of the word as cinematic as this film?' (O.R.-t. 1941, trans.).

The First Division is the film which firmly established Ekman as an important creative force in Swedish cinema. Although it was only his second film, the critics already spoke of him as one of the best. It was praised for the quality of the acting and for the way it expressed itself in cinematic terms. Not all critics were as impressed as the majority, but even the more negative voices were impressed by the cinematography. Furhammar has argued that 'Hasse Ekman is probably the greatest cinematic storyteller we've ever had' (Furhammar 1991: 237, trans.), and the critics at the time seemed to share that assessment. Ekman used editing and camera movement to tell his stories and took advantage of the cinematic elements that make film different from theatre. A moment from *With You in My Arms* exemplifies his editing style: a character is talking and Ekman cuts the scene in the middle of a sentence; in the next shot another character is continuing that sentence at another location. The first half and the second half of the sentence are spoken in two different shots, in different places, at different times, and the link between the two places is the sentence. This is a way of storytelling that Orson Welles made famous in *Citizen Kane* (1941), but Ekman did this before Welles. This, though, is not to argue that Ekman was the first to do it, because it might very well have been done before. Neither is it meant to imply that Ekman influenced Welles, because the possibility that Welles saw *With You in My Arms* is rather slim. They were probably just both thinking along similar lines, independently of one another. Ekman's next film, however, would clearly influence a later film of considerable fame. Ekman's film was called *Flames in the Dark* (*Lågor i dunklet,* 1942) and the film that followed it was *Torment,* written by Ingmar Bergman and directed by Alf Sjöberg.

In *With You in My Arms* a small part was given to Stig Järrel, a Swedish comic actor and friend of Ekman. It was the beginning of a long and mutually beneficial working relationship. In *The First Division* Järrel was given a bigger part and this time a dramatic one, not comic. For *Flames in the Dark* Ekman gave Järrel the leading role. This time it was not merely a dramatic part but a demonic one. The idea for *Flames in the Dark* was partly inspired by the play *Night Must Fall* by Emlyn Williams, and the 1937 film version with the same name, directed by Richard Thorpe. Ekman's script, which he wrote with help from Dagmar Edqvist,[3] tells the story of Birger Sjögren, a sexually and emotionally damaged Latin teacher whose perversions lead to violence and destruction. The role has clear links with Järrel's role in *Torment,* made two years later, where he also plays a conflicted, demonic Latin teacher who frightens and threatens his students.

Flames in the Dark opens with the teacher giving a lecture and becoming more and more intense. Then he is called away as his mother is on her deathbed. It is an emotional death scene, but not in the conventional sense. The mother is partly eager to die, to get away from this world, but at the same time terrified about what will happen to her son when she can no longer protect him from the world and the world from him. Then she dies and the camera focuses on Järrel's face as he walks out of her room and through the apartment, sits down by a telephone and makes a call. Not until after the telephone conversation is there a cut. It is a long, complicated shot of the kind that Ekman had now become an expert in. The rest of the film takes place around Christmas when the teacher is married and has been given a new position at a small school. His jealousy and homicidal tendencies, which he has barely been able to control so far, now break free.

The film was deemed too violent and disturbing by the censors so it was held up for weeks, and the head of the censorship bureau said that it was the most unpleasant film he had seen whilst working as a censor. After a battle in the media, the film was released, with some cuts (Forslund 1982: 157–158). Yet again, the critics were on the whole favourable towards Ekman and the film. In *Stockholms-Tidningen* the reviewer felt that: 'Hasse Ekman continues as a man of surprises, ... Swedish cinema's "kid with the filmic sense"' (Larz 1942, trans.). In *En liten bok om Hasse* Furhammar writes that at the beginning of his career Ekman was treated badly by the film critics (Furhammar & Åhlund 1993: 64) but, as has been shown here, that was not the case.

In 1942 Ekman released two films. After *Flames in the Dark* came *Happiness Approaches* (*Lyckan kommer*), which is a comedy. It again stars Stig Järrel, this time playing a bored businessman who, together with his wife, decides to give up fame and fortune and live in poverty as an artist, fulfilling his dream of becoming a painter. In some ways it is a quintessential Ekman story, partly because of the way a choice is explored between life as an artist and everyday life, and because of the way it addresses Ekman's concern that everyday life can be lifeless and boring, and can destroy a marriage. As will be shown repeatedly throughout this book, the theme of the comfortable life leading to boredom is a central part of Ekman's oeuvre, and the theme of painters and paintings is also a recurring feature of Ekman's work. In addition, *Happiness Approaches*, like the earlier *With You in My Arms*, in the end reaches a kind of anarchic madness complete with false beards and fake Russians which brings to mind the Marx Brothers.

At the end of 1942 Ekman had made four films that had received largely positive reviews and good box-office figures. He had laid the groundwork for what was to come; but before proceeding to discuss what might be considered Ekman's artistic breakthrough, *Changing Trains*, it might be worth summing up Ekman's achievements so far. Ekman had proved that he was a multitalented filmmaker and he had won both the praise of the critics and the love of the crowds. At the annual film critics' award gala in 1942, Ekman won the award for best film, for *The First Division*, and *Flames in the Dark* came in second, tied with a film by Gustaf Molander, *The Battle Goes On* (*Striden går vidare*, 1941). He had demonstrated his deft handling of narrative and his ability to get the most out of his actors. He had shown a willingness to do things differently and he and Stig Järrel had struck up a partnership which was mutually beneficial. Several themes which would eventually become the cornerstones of his art had already been established, such as the question of identities (which is present in three of the films, the exception being *The First Division*), people playing parts and people not showing their true selves, either because they will not or because they cannot. Another theme was a wish to flee the boredom of everyday life and the burden of conformity. Ekman's disregard of, or at least distance from, society's conventions had also been established, even though this is something which would be more pronounced later in his career. And the theme of painters and paintings had been introduced. Stylistically, the films were varied, with the lighting dictated by the story, but two things united them: the use of long takes and an efficient and imaginative editing technique.

In addition to the films already mentioned, Ekman wrote two war-related films in 1943. One was set in the navy and called *Men of the Navy* (*Örlogsmän*) and directed by Börje Larsson. The other was called *Life and Death* (*På liv och död*) and directed by Rolf Husberg. The first is a love story only tangentially related to the war, but the second is a propaganda film set in the north of Sweden about a platoon of alpine riflemen and enemy agents blowing up Swedish troop trains. It ends with a speech given by an officer to his men about the strength of the Swedish military and the importance of being vigilant. However, neither film is of particular interest here, being only marginally concerned with Ekman's usual themes and interests.

So, a number of good and interesting films firmly established Ekman as an important filmmaker in the industry. Yet it was with the next film, *Changing Trains*, that Ekman for the first time showed his full potential, and for the first time told a personal story in a setting he knew well.

As has been said, Ekman was born into the theatre and although his films do not feel theatrical or static he would, from *Changing Trains* onwards, use the theatre as the setting for several of his films. The theatrical world is more than just a setting however, the theatre also has thematic meanings. It is a place of refuge from real life, a haven from the constraints and boredom of petit-bourgeois existence. The theatre, as a place and as a metaphor, is a central aspect of Ekman's work as an auteur. Even in his films with no overt theatre setting there are usually a few scenes at a theatre, or some other performative space, such as a circus or a radio or television station. The treatment of these various performative outlets is not the same, however. Television and radio are ridiculed and are not accorded the same reverence as the theatre. This will be discussed in more detail in chapter 6.

Changing Trains begins with Inga Dahl (Sonja Wigert) coming to a theatre, asking to speak to Leo Waller, the manager/director. He will not have anything to do with her so she leaves and then collapses on the pavement outside the theatre. She is taken to a doctor and told she has a serious heart condition and that she will not live much longer. She decides to go back home. At a train station somewhere in Sweden she accidentally meets Kim Lundell (Ekman), a boy she once loved but gave up for the sake of her theatre career. With Inga and Kim spending the time together until the next train arrives, their story is told in flashbacks. We are moving back and forth in time, between hope and despair, love and betrayal, life and death. The one thing that remains constant is the theatre. In *Changing Trains* the theatre almost has a life of its own. The film breathes the dusty air of dressing rooms, costume wardrobes and the stage (see figure 4.1). The audience gets to see the rehearsals, the backstage discussions, the dressing-room gossip and the anxious wait for the reviews in the morning papers after opening night. Everybody receives some attention, from the manager to the night watchman. In one scene, the theatre's caretaker says, 'I agree with old Frippe, the people of the theatre are all rabble, but they're the only ones you can live with', a line which would be repeated in later films. All these milieus, with scenes such as these, would recur in Ekman's films.

After the opening sequence we are left with a question. Who is this woman, and what is her story? As the film progresses, the audience learns more about her, where she comes from and where she is going. But it is crucial in the film that only the audience is given the full picture of any particular character. The fact that we know more than the characters in the film adds poignancy. The fact that Inga is dying is kept as a secret between us and her. She then continues to act, even if she is no longer on the stage. This time she is acting not for an audience but for Kim. By being untruthful, by playing a part instead of being her true self, she makes him happier than he would otherwise have been.

The film is based on a short novel with the same name, which had come out ten years earlier. When Ekman decided to make a film based on it he met with the writer, Walter Ljungquist, to discuss the project. Ljungquist agreed and filming commenced (Ekman 1955: 154–155). It would be the first of several films they made together. It should be noted that there are many differences between the source novel and the finished film, changes which reveal something about Ekman's concerns and ideas. One such idea, or perhaps philosophy, is the conscious effort to try and evade the unpleasant aspects of life and to hang on to the

Figure 4.1: Inga Dahl (Sonja Wigert) and people of the theatre in *Changing Trains*. Photo courtesy of Studio S Entertainment. Image from the Swedish Film Institute Archives.

good parts – the beautiful, precious things that make it all worthwhile. In the film, contrary to the book, Inga never tells anyone that she has a heart condition and is going to die soon; she keeps that to herself. Towards the end, Kim tells Inga that they must 'forget about everything, and just be really happy'. Of course, that sentiment will only take them so far. But the most important change from book to film is the expansion of the story and the change of focus from Kim (in the book) to Inga (in the film). In the book there are no flashbacks, no tales about the theatre and no Leo Waller. Whilst it is true that Inga is an actor in the book, this is only mentioned in passing a few times: this is not what the book is about. In the film, she and her theatre career are given more scrutiny.

The film is not, however, only about the theatre. It is also about Ekman. The leading character in the film is the woman, Inga Dahl, but it is through the men that Ekman touches on the more personal issues. Bengt Forslund has argued that Leo Waller, the 'Great Actor' and creative force of the theatre, has strong similarities to Ekman's father, Gösta Ekman (Forslund 1982: 164), whereas Ekman has stated that Kim, the young man, is a portrait of himself (Ekman 1955: 155), an analogy which is, perhaps obviously, emphasised by the fact that he plays the part himself. Inga, on the other hand, was inspired by the Norwegian-Swedish actress Tutta Rolf, with whom Ekman for most of the 1930s had been deeply in love, without it being reciprocated (Ekman 1955: 155; Forslund 1982: 202–203). This resonance is also emphasised by the fact that Inga is played by Wigert, a Norwegian actress who came to Sweden in 1939. Whereas Forslund may have argued that Leo Waller was Ekman's portrait of his father, Ekman in his autobiography *Den vackra ankungen* stipulates that Waller was a portrait of his rival for Tutta Rolf's affections, the American Jack Donohue (Ekman 1955: 155). This is not to suggest that what happens to the characters in the film is based on what happened in real life, but rather that the film can be seen as an allegory for the triangle Ekman, Rolf and Donohue found themselves in, and that the film is full of possible autobiographical readings.

The first time Kim is seen he is leaving his home and his parents because he is going to South America. It is clear that he has a strained relationship with his father and that his wish to get away from it all is strong. It is the first of many complex father-and-son relationships and, without doing a psychoanalytic analysis of Ekman and his films, it is worth pointing out that this is a recurring motif in Ekman's work. Also noteworthy is the fact that Ekman has changed the destination for Kim's trip. In the book he is going to Sumatra, one of the Indonesian islands, but in the film he is going to South America. This is not the only allusion to South America in Ekman's films, since longing for that continent connects most of his leading characters. But why South America?

As was mentioned in the introduction, during the second half of the nineteenth century and the first half of the twentieth century an immense number of Swedes emigrated to the USA and to a lesser extent Australia. But a substantial number also went to South America, in particular Brazil and Argentina. The reasons why Swedes emigrated were the poverty and the harsh weather conditions in Sweden, with the plains of Brazil and Argentina evoking the appeal of rich, warm and fertile land. At this time, Brazil and Argentina were developing fast, becoming modern nations, so it was not just the poor who went, but professional engineers and artists, most famously perhaps the singer and poet Evert Taube. The strong connections between Sweden and South America continued to exist, even after Sweden became rich and prosperous in its own right and emigration ended. Ekman invoked South America with such regularity partly because of this cultural history and partly because it represented warmth and a more relaxed way of life, regardless of whether this relaxed lifestyle was mythical or real. But as with the theatre, South America also becomes a metaphor for the need for escape from everyday life, from the same constraints and restrictions that all his main characters fear, and from which many of them suffer

It seems clear that *Changing Trains* meant something special for Ekman. He chose the source, and transformed it into something unique and personal. After having shown that he knew the craft of filmmaking, he now showed that he was also an artist, with something to say. He had something to share with the audience. Unfortunately, his first audience consisted of one man, Lorens Marmstedt, the producer, and he was most dissatisfied. Marmstedt felt that Ekman had been too influenced by French filmmakers such as Renoir and Carné and that Ekman and Sonja Wigert were not exactly Jean Gabin and Michèle Morgan, try as they might (Ekman 1955: 156). In terms of its general mood, *Changing Trains* does give the impression of having been influenced by Carné and Jacques Prévert, as were Bergman and several other Swedish filmmakers at the time. A feeling of sadness, of a shadow of death hanging over the characters, is palpable. Occasionally the look of the film, especially in the end, also brings to mind the French school: the use of rain and mist and an expressionistic but simultaneously subdued use of shadow are among the visual traits that link Ekman's film with French predecessors.[4] Yet though there are visual links, the film is still a unique work as it is filled with Ekman's personal concerns, not to mention the links between the film and Ekman's own life. Even though Marmstedt had his concerns, when the film critics voted for best Swedish film of the season *Changing Trains* won. Alf Sjöberg's *The Heavenly Play* came in second (Forslund 1982: 164). Ekman could feel confident that making something so personal would pay off.

Changing Trains is also important because it was the first time Ekman worked with the cinematographer Göran Strindberg and the editor Lennart Wallén. Ekman and Strindberg would make five films together, and while *Changing Trains* is not as stylish – it often looks like a low-budget production – their later films together are among Ekman's visually most accomplished, not least as far as lighting is concerned. Strindberg would photograph an impressive number of the most notable Swedish films of the 1940s and early 1950s, working with Bergman on several, with Sjöberg on *Miss Julie* and with Mattsson on *One Summer of Happiness*, among others. Wallén on the other hand was one of Sweden's most accomplished editors and after *Changing Trains* he and Ekman made twenty films together. Ekman's imaginative use of associative editing had been in place already from his first film, so whether Wallén introduced something new to Ekman's films is debatable. However, since Ekman was a filmmaker who was very conscious of the power of editing and used it so creatively, working closely with the same editor must have been invaluable.

By this point, Ekman can be said to have fulfilled all the requirements of an auteur. Although his oeuvre as yet amounted to only five films, the consistencies were considerable and this despite working in different genres and with different crews. *Changing Trains* also firmly establishes Ekman as an internal auteur, one who makes his own life part of the film and who plays an active part before as well as behind the camera. Barthes may have claimed that 'it is language which speaks, not the author' (Barthes 1977: 143), but only the author would be able to tell personal stories and it is often the ideas and obsessions of the author that make one individual film different from all other films. Language and discourse matter, but they are not all that matters: individuals are essential too. At the same time, it is also clear that what interests Ekman are people, individuals, rather than the nation or history.

Following *Changing Trains*, Marmstedt suggested that Ekman's next film should be the circus melodrama *The Sixth Shot* (*Det sjätte skottet*, 1943), with a Continental setting. It was not written by Ekman but by Gösta Stevens, who usually worked with Gustaf Molander. It was even presented as: 'A film by Gösta

Stevens' in the title sequence. Although the film as a whole is not particularly interesting, it has interesting moments. The opening scene takes place in Monte Carlo, where a man is on the verge of suicide. An unknown woman appears by his side and starts to talk to him without any inhibitions. It turns out that the man has had a difficult life, with a stormy relationship with his father, and when the father died he sold everything and moved abroad. Now he has come to the end of his rope, with no money left. But instead of killing himself as was his plan, he strikes up a partnership with the woman in the circus world.

Yet again the leading couple are played by Edvin Adolphson and Karin Ekelund, and as should be relatively clear by now, the opening sequence has many typical Ekman ingredients, such as the complex father–son relationship and the wish to get out into the world. The film also has a strong, assertive woman in the lead, a recurring character in Ekman's films. There is a feminist side to Ekman's films, and they are filled with women who want to be in control of their own destinies, who take charge even though the world is often ruled by sexist or cruel men.

But the bulk of the films Ekman made in 1943 and 1944 were connected to the war. *A Day Will Come* was set during the Winter War in Finland, *An Occupation for Men* (*Ett yrke för män*, 1944) was a short film about the army, and *His Excellency* (*Excellensen*, 1944) was an existential drama revolving around the Nazi persecution of an intellectual. Ekman also made a film about life in an office in wartime Stockholm, *Common People* (*Som folk är mest*, 1944), which was in a lighter mood albeit with serious undertones.

A Day Will Come, scripted by Ekman together with Sven Stolpe, has Edvin Adolphson in the leading role, while Ekman also stars. The film tries to strike a balance between propaganda and subdued anti-war film with some success, but its greatest assets are the impressive visuals, both in the interior sequences and in the vistas and battle scenes (the cinematographer is Olle Nordemar, and this was the only film he made with Ekman). It tells the story of an assorted collection of Swedish soldiers who have joined up to fight with the Finnish against the Soviet Union. Of the main characters, one (Adolphson) is a fugitive from justice and another (Ekman) is from the nobility but has broken with his family, who consider him no good. During the war they both rise to the occasion but life at the front takes its toll, and they must battle guilt, alcohol abuse and anxiety attacks, as well as the opposing troops. In the end both are killed by enemy fire.

His Excellency is very different. It is not set at the front line but is more of a chamber play, scripted not by Ekman but by Stolpe, and based on a play by Bertil

Malmberg. A famous writer and public intellectual, Herbert von Blankenau (Lars Hanson), is seen by the rising Nazi Party as an enemy and after the Nazis take power he is captured and sent to a concentration camp. But his moral authority and beliefs make it impossible for the Nazis to break him. In a battle between moral superiority and raw power, morality triumphs. Even though von Blankenau is finally shot and killed, his example inspires the resistance. When the prison commandant, who is not German but from the occupied country, witnesses Blankenau's firm humanistic and democratic outlook, and the strength Blankenau gains from this moral certainty, the commandant is first puzzled but then succumbs to this moral certainty himself and goes from being a committed Nazi to becoming a resistance fighter. It is not clear where the film is set, but in the original play both the country, Austria, and the concentration camp, Buchenwald, are named. Due to censorship rules in Sweden the locations were kept anonymous, otherwise it would not have been possible for the film to be released.

The critics were pleased with the fact that *His Excellency* not only had been made but could actually be shown. In *Svensk film under andra världskriget* (Olsson 1979), the film is given a lot of attention and Olsson goes as far as to suggest that *His Excellency* is one of the most important works of art made during the war. It is certainly unique in a Swedish context for its outspokenness against Nazism, even though the names have been withheld. It is also another example of the interest Ekman had in people and their drives and motives. *His Excellency* is about the importance of the individual and the freedom of that individual and this is something that all of Ekman's characters can relate to. All wish to be free to pursue their own dreams. Few are under threat so much as Blankenau, but the principle is the same. This will be discussed further in chapter 7.

Yet *A Day Will Come* and *His Excellency* are still somewhat unusual in form and content for Ekman. His next film, *Common People*, was more traditionally Ekman-esque. He signed a new contract making him head of production, which meant that he had considerable freedom as a filmmaker but would also take full responsibility for the production. He is credited as writer, director and producer and so must have had almost complete control. However, the script is not an original but based on three different one-act plays by Herbert Grevenius. Grevenius was a leading playwright and theatre critic at the time, and he also worked with Bergman occasionally.

In *His Excellency* Stig Järrel had played a cruel Nazi officer; in *Common People* Järrel returned, but this time as Enander, a cruel office manager at an office in

Stockholm, complete with a Hitler moustache. The film concerns the employees at the office, their everyday dreams and hopes and aspirations, constantly living in fear of Järrel's watchful eye and the threat of unemployment and poverty. The film begins with a sequence of shots showing the main characters waking up in the morning, and the different ways they react to the alarm clock. Here in one brief montage Ekman introduces not only the characters but also the main theme of the film: the conflict between spontaneity and rigidity (for example, Enander is seen sitting in bed with a wristwatch in his hand, impatiently waiting for the alarm clock to go off). In the centre is a young couple, Inga and Kurre, who want to get married but since they do not earn enough money are reluctant to do so. At work life is difficult, especially since Enander, the office manager, is so unforgiving and strict, keeping an eye on everybody and reprimanding them if they are a minute late. The office has glass walls and through the use of deep-focus cinematography, Enander can be seen moving around in the background of the shot, his presence felt even when he is not part of the scene. He has a scientific mind and has a mantra which he often repeats; having a method is key for everything. Inga works at 'his' office and one of the storylines in the film is the conflict between them. This is introduced by the kind of cut that is typical of Ekman. In the beginning of the film, Inga is seen entering a room and closing a door behind her. As soon as the door is shut, Ekman cuts to a shot of another door just as it is about to be opened by Enander, followed by him entering another room. Even though they have not been properly introduced yet, nor has their relation to each other been established, the two characters are linked visually through this cut, which also shows the opposition between them. If she closes a door, he opens it.

Another storyline is the frustration and boredom that both Kurre and Inga feel with their present condition. At one point a friend of Kurre says that Inga is rather attractive, to which Kurre replies: 'Is she? I've stopped noticing that, since I see her all the time'. In another scene Inga comes home, tired and exasperated after a bad day at the office. After sitting with her head in her hands she puts on a record and slowly begins dancing with herself, her back to the camera, dreaming of just fleeing her existence. She does not say where she would like to go, but Kurre at one point talks longingly about moving to 'South America, the land of the future'.

But in the end all is resolved satisfactorily and even the cruel manager shows a human side after accidentally getting drunk at the office party, together with the watchman. It is a typical Swedish solution perhaps, with everybody getting along and class distinctions becoming blurred; a positive message for the home front. But at the same time, when Inga and Kurre resolve their differences during a night when they are trapped in a lift at her office, the film ends with her saying that she would prefer to stay at home and try to make things work rather then move away, with the words: 'This is good enough'. It is not exactly a passionate sentiment but rather more realistic. The film addresses many of Ekman's concerns, and he clearly links a fanatic attention to orderliness, efficiency and time management – a 'scientisation' of society – with fascism. Unfortunately, *Common People* has barely registered in the annals of Swedish cinema. It is not even mentioned in the one book written specifically about Ekman, Furhammar's *En liten bok om Hasse*. In a way it is not that surprising since the film is an unassuming comedy of manners. But it is also interesting for its acutely observed scenes from the daily lives of ordinary Swedes and it is rather moving. This is an example of how, by focusing on ordinary people, without having to introduce strong drama, tragedy or action, it is possible to capture a specific time and place, and in so doing tell a story that is more than simply about the individuals in the film. This is the kind of film that the majority of the audience in 1944 would have been able to relate to, and at the same time it today becomes a document not only of cinema at the time, but of society, regardless of whether this was intended or not. With its focus, *Common People* could be said to be the first part of an unofficial *folkhem* trilogy by Ekman, with the other two being *While the Door Was Looked* (*Medan porten var stängd*, 1946) and *We Three Debutantes* (*Vi tre debutera*, 1953), the last of which was also based on the writings of Herbert Grevenius. The view of society grows more ambivalent from film to film, which will be discussed later.

Another important film from 1944 was one Ekman neither wrote nor directed: *Stop! Thing about Something Else* (*Stopp! Tänk på något annat*). It was written by Olle Hedberg and directed by Åke Ohberg, and is an ambitious drama about two young lovers, movingly played by Ekman and Eva Henning. It is the pairing of the two that makes the film important because not only were they very good together, they also began a professional as well as personal relationship, and for the rest of the decade they would be a team. Henning made comparatively few films, and primarily with three directors, Ohberg, Ekman and Bergman. But it is for her films with Ekman that she has become famous.

The next year, 1945, was an important year. The war ended, and in the Swedish film world Ingmar Bergman made his first film as writer and director. Things would rapidly change from then on, and to a large extent for the better. It would be one of Ekman's most successful years, artistically as well as commercially. These were also exhausting times for Ekman. In his autobiography he writes of how, around midsummer 1944, he collapsed on a chair and thought: 'It cannot go on like this! For sixteen months I have directed four feature films, one short film and one theatre play: I have played four parts and written three scripts. ... This has got to stop, this has definitely got to stop!' (Ekman 1955: 164, trans.). In view of this quote it might come as a surprise that after this he made three films in a row, from late autumn of 1944 until the summer of 1945. Even more surprising perhaps is that those three films were so successful, all gained very good reviews and are today considered among Ekman's very best. To call 1945 a peak year would not be hyperbole.

The first of these is *Royal Rabble* (*Kungliga patrasket*, 1945). It was a film Ekman was eager to make, and allegedly he wrote a large part of it at his favourite bar, Cecil's, because he did not have a home at this point (ibid.: 171). (Cecil's bar, which will appear again later in this chapter, was also where Ekman and Stig Järrel developed the character Birger, the Latin teacher in *Flames in the Dark*.) *Royal Rabble* is Ekman's second theatre film and, like *Changing Trains*, a film with auto-biographical elements, or at least a family resemblance. It is the story of the theatre family Anker and was the first time Ekman introduced the Anker family to his audience. From then on, characters with the name 'Anker' would appear from time to time in Ekman's films, whenever there was a theatre setting. It is tempting to see the Anker family as a screen version of the Ekman family, but sometimes the connections are more tenuous than real. In *Royal Rabble*, however, the similarities should be noted. It is one of the most explicit examples of Ekman as an internal auteur. The cinematographer was Hilding Bladh, this being the sixth of the ten films he and Ekman made together. It is not their finest work, but it has coherence and an intimate lighting style.

At its centre is Stefan Anker, the great actor and head of the family. The family consists of his wife Betty, his children Tommy and Monica and his parents Karl-Hugo and Charlotta. The film follows them, much like in *Changing Trains*, through rehearsals, script readings, opening nights and nightly vigils, waiting for the arrival of the reviews, as well as getting in and out of costume and makeup. As in *Changing Trains*, the theatre almost becomes a character in its own right. To add to the interconnections between the films, the title of *Royal Rabble* refers to the line from *Changing Trains*, quoted above, about the people of the theatre being 'all rabble'. While espousing this romantic view of the theatre, the film also looks at the strains that the theatre life puts on the family, and especially the egomania of Stefan Anker. The critical point comes when he has an affair with a young starlet.

Royal Rabble received very good reviews when it was released in January of 1945. It was perhaps, from a critical perspective, Ekman's most successful film to date. One leading critic, Stig Almqvist, wrote: 'If ever a Swedish film has been the work of one man, it is Royal Rabble. Had the result been less good, all criticism would have been directed against Hasse: now on the other hand it is he who will be covered in flowers more than anyone else' (Almqvist 1945, trans.). And most critics noticed the similarities between the family Anker, especially Stefan Anker, and the Ekman family and Gösta Ekman.

The opening of the film takes place after an evening's performance and all the actors and the members of the Anker family are changing back into everyday clothes. It is like a montage of short scenes from one dressing room after another, while in his office the great actor is preparing for interviews and meetings with writers and actors who seek to be hired by him. Long after all the other family members have gone home and to bed, Stefan Anker leaves the theatre. When he comes home, late in the night, he wakes everybody up so they can have a meeting in the kitchen. Whilst he is making lamb chops, he talks about his idea for the next project for their theatre.

When Gösta Ekman died in 1938, a book was published to honour his memory. Several people who had worked with him, and members of his own family, wrote essays and shared their memories about him. Hasse Ekman was among those who contributed and in his essay he wrote (among other things):

> *Never again will I see him, never again will I hear his voice. Never again will I sit on a chair out in the kitchen on Artillerigatan [Artillery Street] at two o'clock in the morning and listen to his elaborations on plays, roles, projects and rehearsals, while he himself is standing by the stove with a pan in one hand and a list of parts in the other.*
>
> *I hear him say*
>
> *- Whatever I might know, I do know how to fry a lamb chop.* (Ekman 1938: 5, trans.)

That is the scene, almost word for word, that was described above. So it is clear that Ekman, when writing *Royal Rabble*, was drawing on real-life events – some well known, others more private and some perhaps unintentional. That is not to say that Stefan Anker and Gösta Ekman are the same person, but such a reading is possible. Or rather, the connections between the real man and the fictional character are so clear that failing to draw attention to them would be a mistake.

As he usually did, Ekman also played a part in *Royal Rabble*: Tommy Anker, the son of Stefan Anker. As was mentioned earlier, in *Intermezzo* Ekman played the son and his own father, Gösta, played the father. Here, Ekman played the role of the son of his fictionalised father, and the actor playing the father was the one actor who had been like a father figure for Ekman during his own career, Edvin Adolphson. (It should be mentioned that Ekman was still fairly young: he was only twenty-nine when he made *Royal Rabble*.) In *Intermezzo* there is a scene in which father and son are having an argument about the father always being absent, never taking an interest in the family. Similar scenes are to be found in *Royal Rabble*. Also, in the opening sequence the following dialogue between the son and a fellow actor takes place in their dressing room:

> Rolf: *I think Ibsen is overrated. Now, if you compare him to Strindberg…*
> Tommy: *Why do you have to compare? I think it is silly.*
> Rolf: *Said the son who does not want to be compared to his great father.*

This dialogue is rich in connotation but there is no need to go further here than to point out the mood of art imitating life.

Royal Rabble was the first film Ekman directed which had Eva Henning in it, and she would from then on be his leading lady. In *Royal Rabble* she did not play the lead, however; that came first with Ekman's next film of 1945, *Wandering with the Moon* (*Vandring med månen*). This film, which Ekman made in the spring of 1945, was the second collaboration between Ekman and the writer Walter Ljungquist. This time Ekman was for the first time not working at Terra with Marmstedt but for the rival studio, SF. The book was called *Vandring med månen* and the film kept the title and had its premiere in August of 1945. The reason Ekman was working for SF instead of Terra was that SF owned the rights to *Vandring med månen*, and the new head of production at SF wanted Ekman to make it into a film. Ekman agreed to do it on condition that he could give a part to the actress Eva Henning and work together with Ljungquist on the script, to which SF agreed (Forslund 1982: 174).

Wandering with the Moon tells the story of a young man, Dan, who has a fraught relationship with his father and after a heated argument in which Dan says 'I can't stand you. I can't stand myself, and I can't stand my office', he decides to leave home and go abroad. He is walking along a deserted country road, talking to the moon, when a bus with a travelling theatre group comes along and the driver asks for directions. One of the actresses, Pia, jumps off the bus and asks Dan if she may walk with him and, hesitantly, he says yes. For the rest of the film we follow them, walking, talking and meeting various characters on the way over the course of a few days. It is not a film with a clear, linear structure but rather an episodic, lyrical narrative. It is also a film about innocence and innocence lost; and, which often goes hand in hand with this, virginity and sexual inexperience. The first night Pia says to Dan: 'Do you want to be my lover? I've never been with another man'. He cannot deal with this revelation; the thought of her and possibly himself as sexual beings makes him uncomfortable and even disgusted. But at the end of the film she finally makes him succumb, and they are both in a sense liberated. The beginning of the film is reminiscent of the beginning of *The Sixth Shot* in that a woman approaches a strange and unhappy man and by befriending him gives him a reason to live, a sense that life has more to offer than they thought. It should also be added that their walk together in the beginning is shot in one long take and that the sequence is repeated in the last scene of the film – yet another example of how Ekman links the beginning and the end together, here with Dan walking along a country road, talking to the moon. The difference is that whereas he was alone in the first scene, in the last scene he is with Pia.

Dan and Pia meet many different characters along the way and it is illuminating to look more closely at some of them. On his own Dan first meets a vagabond, played by Stig Järrel. The vagabond has an ironic and open-minded approach to life and misery. A poet and a philosopher, he takes things as they come and argues that nothing is important; that he himself is an insignificant being, one 'whose name is written in running water', as he puts it. However, he praises the youth and is anxious for the couple to get a head start, before they too become cynical. This is the one thing that connects the various characters Dan and Pia encounter: the wish to protect and/or pity the young for the experienced know that the idealism and hope of the young will inevitably give way to the cynicism and disappointment of adulthood and maturity.

They meet a careworn old woman (played by Hjördis Pettersson) who is the keeper of an inn where they spend the night, and she tells them that only those who gamble in life will really live. They also meet a priest (Hilding Gavle), who, when Dan confesses that he is an atheist, says: 'Well, I prefer an honest atheist to a dishonest Christian'. But another piece of advice that everyone they meet gives is that in order to get ahead in life, they need to learn to use masks, to hide their true identities, because, as a man played by Ekman says: 'Everybody walks around with a mask'. The woman at the inn says that in order to remain sane and be able to function in the world '[y]ou must always try and be something other than you really are' and use irony as an escape mechanism. At one point when Dan is exasperated with all the hopelessness and cynicism he encounters, he demands to know if there is no belief in goodness, to be told: yes, there is goodness, but it is so desperately fragile. Yet despite these sometimes uncomfortable truths, most of the people they meet see something hopeful in the love and idealism that Dan and Pia radiate. It is as if these people become spokespersons for different ideas, for Ekman's view of life, as they speak of the need to hide behind masks, of the apparent inevitability of cynicism and boredom, and how experience and conformity stifle life. At the same time there is also hope: the hope of breaking free from conventions and traditions, for example by devoting oneself to the arts, in particular the theatre. These themes, together with the loose narrative and the poetic imagery, make this film a good example of the similarities between Ekman and Jean Renoir, and their shared sensibility.

Wandering with the Moon received good reviews. According to the film critic and historian, Bengt Idestam-Almquist, writing under the name Robin Hood: 'Wandering with the Moon has poetry. That is its great allure' (Hood 1945, trans.). That remains one of the main strengths of the film and part of that is due to the episodic structure and the lyrical images of the countryside. The cinematographer this time was Gösta Roosling, who hardly ever worked on feature films. His expertise was in newsreels and documentaries of people and nature. It is possible that Ekman chose him for this reason.

The third and last film Ekman made in 1945 was *Little Märta Steps Forward* (*Fram för lilla Märta*). It was a much more light-hearted film, shot during the summer and with its premiere on 29 September 1945. Since working at SF on *Wandering with the Moon* was an anomaly, Ekman was back at Terra. *Little Märta Steps Forward* would turn out to be Terra's greatest financial success so far (Forslund 1982: 176), so they were probably very happy about Ekman's return.

Ekman wrote the script specifically with Järrel in mind for the title character. It is the story of two male musicians who, because of financial distress, decide to apply for a job in an all-female orchestra. Sture (Järrel) gets the job posing as a woman, 'Märta', and Kurre (Ekman) comes along too, posing as 'her' fiancé. They each fall in love with female members of the orchestra, but Sture, once he starts playing the part of a woman, also starts to think like one. It is not long before s/he becomes upset by the treatment of women and eventually becomes the local candidate in the national election, on a feminist ticket, still playing the role of Märta. Once elected, s/he gives a rousing speech in parliament, urging them to abolish laws which are detrimental to women and make new, progressive laws instead. It is a very interesting film and again the theme of the film is role playing and play-acting, and the way that the role we are playing determines our personality, or, perhaps, that our personalities are fluent and shifting, depending upon the circumstances.

The film is a comedy, and it is rather hesitant even from the start. The first title card reads 'Terrafilm presents', the next card reads 'somewhat reluctantly', and yet another card mentions 'the so-called plot'. But despite this playfulness, the suffering of some of the female characters is sincerely felt and the film does raise interesting questions, which are in keeping with one of Ekman's pet themes, the elusiveness of identity. *Little Märta Steps Forward* received great reviews. The feminist and occasional film critic Barbro Alving, writing under the name Bang, wrote: 'As a grey-haired champion of the female cause and a sincere citizen I welcome little Märta Letterström from Lillköping with all my heart as our pitiful community is so short on public figures with initiative, force and charisma. A handful of women like this and the Swedish parliament can close shop' (Bang 1945, trans.).

The story has an unusual framing device. It is set in the future, where an old man and a young girl drive past Lillköping, the (fictional) town where the main story takes place. They stop in the centre and the old man shows a big statue to the young girl. It is a statue of Märta, the pride of Lillköping. In a brave new world, women might perhaps eventually be the rulers. This is another example of Ekman's feminist side, and although it is a light-hearted film, the oppression of women would be dealt with in a darker mood later in Ekman's career.

That concludes Ekman's first years as a filmmaker, the war years. Those were extraordinary years for Swedish cinema in general and for Ekman in particular. The immediate post-war era would also be remarkable and the next section will deal with this period. This was when Ekman solidified his position in Swedish film culture but it was also when he suddenly found himself with a rival: Ingmar

Bergman. So far it has been possible to discuss Ekman without reference to Ingmar Bergman. That is no longer the case, because by this time not only had Bergman become a powerful presence in Swedish cinema, but his and Ekman's collaboration had started, as had their rivalry.

One of the key aspects of Ekman's filmmaking career is that, unlike almost any other Swedish director before the 1960s, he made hardly any films set in the countryside. It might be argued that Ekman was the only completely urban film-maker in Sweden at the time, and for several decades to come. *Wandering with the Moon* and *Little Märta Steps Forward* are two lone exceptions. Additionally, he made only two films that were set in the past: *The Jazz Boy* and his last film, *The Marriage Wrestler* (*Äktenskapsbrottaren*, 1964). His was a cinema of the here and now, and of the city. As was mentioned in chapter 3, rural films were one of the most popular types in Sweden, and the 'summer films' were almost a genre in their own right. A prime example was *One Summer of Happiness*, but many of Bergman's films in the 1950s were 'summer films' as well, like *Summer Interlude* (*Sommarlek*, 1951) and *Summer with Monika* (*Sommaren med Monica*, 1953). Schamyl Bauman made most of his films in a rural setting, or in the archipelago, which was signalled in their titles, such as *Rospiggar* (1942; the title is the Swedish name for those who live in Roslagen, a rural area just north of Stockholm). *In Darkest Småland* (*I mörkaste Småland*, 1943) and its sequel, *The Girls in Småland* (*Flickorna i Småland*, 1945), refer to Småland, which is a rural area in the south of Sweden. By contrast, with the exception of the above-mentioned films and the war film *A Day Will Come*, Ekman stayed clear of life outside the big cities and when a film did partly take place in a provincial town, the town was criticised for being boring, small minded and full of gossip. One reason for this is that, judging by his films, Ekman had a sophisticated view of the world: he was tolerant and modern, and this worldview was easier to accommodate in a big city than in the countryside. Another recurring theme in his films is the fear of boredom and stag-nation and this is perhaps something more likely to happen in the countryside than in the city. His strong interest in the artistic world is another reason why it feels natural that his films should be so urban, given the norms of Swedish cinema. Yet another reason for this urbanity is that Ekman preferred to make films about milieus he was familiar with, and about people that he knew. He once said, referring to himself in third person, that: 'He did not like to work in milieus that he did not know, had not seen; he did not like to deal with characters that he had not shaken hands with, had never offered a cigarette to or asked what time it was; it made him feel insecure' (Ekman 1955: 162, trans.). Even though Ekman had made several successful films about characters far from his own world (such as *The First Division*, about pilots in the air force), he usually kept his films close to home. This urbanity is one of the stronger claims for him as an auteur (and is where he differs from Renoir, who seems to have a more romantic idea of nature and the countryside).

As has already been established, Ekman was a prolific filmmaker, as were most of his peers. In 1946 he wrote and directed three films, and he played a leading role in all of them. That year also saw the premiere of a film he wrote but which was directed by Rolf Husberg, called *Love and Downhill Racing*. The film is on one level a banal love story but since it is self-consciously treated as such by Ekman's script it becomes a metafilmic experience, a film that is about its own making and that also makes fun of itself and its maker(s). Therefore, this section will begin by a discussion of *Love and Downhill Racing* and how it works together with the idea of Ekman as an auteur, even though he did not direct it. In the very positive reviews, Husberg's name is not mentioned, only those of Ekman and his co-writer, Sven Björkman.

Love and Downhill Racing begins at a film set, where the writer and the director are having an argument about a piece of dialogue which the director has changed without informing the writer. The film then follows the writer's travails as he wants to make a film version of August Strindberg's play 'Erik IVX', about the Swedish king from the mid-1500s, but the producers insist that he write something commercial and playful, like a romantic comedy set in the north of Sweden. In a reference to the fierce competition between the studios already alluded to, the writer says: 'well, fortunately there are other production companies one can go to'. But eventually he gives in to the idea of writing the romantic comedy, and takes the train to the cold and snow-covered north, having been convinced by the producer that no expense will be spared and that he will feel 'just as comfortable as if you were at Cecil's bar'. Cecil's bar was famously Ekman's favourite bar in Stockholm and this is but one allusion among many to the fact that this particular fictional scriptwriter and Ekman, the actual scriptwriter, are related. What then follows is a series of confusions and mistaken identities, including a battle of the sexes between the writer and a journalist from a gossip magazine. They eventually fall for each other, and in the last scene they embrace on his bed.

The last scene is typical of Ekman's storytelling, even if this film was not directed by him. It is almost exactly like the first scene of the film, which also concerns two lovers embracing on a bed. The dialogue is also similar. This is how many of Ekman's films are constructed. As already mentioned, *The First Division* and *Wandering with the Moon* begin and end with similar scenes. *Royal Rabble* and *Little Märta Steps Forward* are further examples of the way in which Ekman likes to make the last scene a repetition of the first, but with some significant difference. In so doing, it could be argued that he manages to show how life has no clear beginnings and endings, that there is a sense of continuity, regardless of people's activities. At the same time, since there is a subtle difference on an individual level between the beginning and the end, it also shows that although life, or the world, is bigger than the individuals who inhabit it, those individuals still have their own, very important lives – important for them, even though they may not be important in the larger scheme of things. This is a key element in Ekman's films, and as more of his films are discussed, more examples of this will be given.

The three films from 1946 that Ekman wrote, directed and starred in are *Meeting in the Night* (*Möte i natten*), *Waiting Room for Death* and *While the Door Was Locked* and they are all very singular films. Only the third is a traditional Ekman film, but for different reasons they are all of interest. *Waiting Room for Death* was a film that Ekman made partly as a favour to the producer Lorens Marmstedt. Ekman wrote the script together with Walter Ljungquist and it is clearly inspired by Thomas Mann's novel *The Magic Mountain* (*Die Zauberberg*, 1924), although it is based upon a novel by the Swedish writer Sven Stolpe. Stolpe had collaborated with Ekman on the two war films, *A Day Will Come* and *His Excellency*, but this time Stolpe did not want to have anything to do with the finished film (Forslund 1982: 177). This would be the eighth of the ten films Hilding Bladh shot for Ekman, and with its carefully and elaborately lit interiors it is the peak of their cooperation. (see figure 4.2)

The setting is a sanatorium in Switzerland and the main character is played by Ekman. He plays a young man from Sweden sent there, as he believes, to relax, not realising that he is actually very ill. There he meets several other patients from around the world and he also becomes attached to a free-spirited woman, who, even though she is very sick, would rather live life as passionately as she can instead of following the advice of her doctor to stay in her room, literally waiting for death. That character must have appealed to Ekman. Part of the appeal for Marmstedt in making the film probably had to do with his passion for European filmmaking, of which there would be more examples later in his career. (This will be discussed in the next chapter.)

Figure 4.2: A death in *Waiting Room for Death*. Photo courtesy of Studio S Entertainment. Image from the Swedish Film Institute Archives.

The next film Ekman made was the thriller *Meeting in the Night*. The plot concerns a journalist's attempt to expose the dreadful conditions in the Swedish prison system by faking a crime and seeing to it that he gets locked up. The plan is that he will pretend to kill a friend in a fit of jealousy, and then while the friend goes into hiding the journalist will go to the police and confess. Then, after a month, the friend will go to the police and they will explain everything. However, after the journalist has been convicted his friend is actually murdered and the body found and since nobody else knew about the hoax, the journalist no longer has any hopes of being set free. Instead, he escapes from prison and tries to find the killer himself. Ekman was most unhappy about making it, as he felt it was contrived and not believable (Ekman 1955: 182–183). Being a professional, he completed it but it does sometimes feel like it is a parody of thrillers more than anything else. Some sequences are very playful and there are several dialogue scenes that might as well have come from one of his comedies. It is tempting to see this as another example of what Ekman did with *Love and Downhill Racing*. When asked to do something he did not want to do he wrote the script as a parody, in a very self-conscious way.

Yet even if Ekman's heart was not in it, and even if the thriller aspects do not really work, one joy of the film is the dialogue, and this is the case for the whole of Ekman's career. The first noticeable thing about his dialogue, at least for some-body who understands Swedish, is that it sounds natural. In too many Swedish films of this time the words either come across as overtly stagy or laughable. But Ekman wrote for film, not the theatre, and he made his characters speak in a realistic way, in terms of both how they spoke and what they said. It is a combina-tion of writing and directing of course, as the diction does not come from the page but from the acting and directing. One critic wrote in 1949 that: 'his dia-logue, the wonderful, living, natural, agile and acutely interpreted dialogue [is] probably the best dramatic dialogue that anybody is writing in this country, besides Herbert Grevenius' (Tannefors 1949, trans.).

And there is more to the dialogue than its verisimilitude. Ekman also gives the impression of being in love with words, accents, dialects and phrasing. One of the things he does in *Meeting in the Night* is to allow his various characters to speak in a baffling variety of slang, some almost incomprehensible, and he uses this for comic effects. There is a telephone conversation that has an almost surreal quality due to the play with dialects and words. Mikaela Kindblom has written that: 'the dialogue in an Hasse Ekman film is on the whole filled with an enthusiastic wish to explore the resources and capabilities of words and language' (Kindblom 2004, trans.), and she also mentions the way certain words sometimes feel like they have a life of their own. To that can be added that it sometimes feels like both Ekman and his characters are amused and amazed by these words. In one scene in his film *Girl with Hyacinths* a husband and wife start an argument over the meaning of a particular word that the man has just used and which neither of them actually understands. This is a perfect example of this love of words that Ekman exhibits. There is also more to it than just how words and dialogue are used in themselves. As exemplified in *With You in My Arms*, Ekman also plays with dialogue for narra-tive purposes, for example by splitting a sentence between two different settings, or having a question asked in one scene answered in another scene, in another setting and at some other time. Words for Ekman can play many different roles.

Words can also hurt. *Meeting in the Night* led to a well-publicised feud between Ekman and the critic Robin Hood, which would have lasting effects on

Ekman and his future career. Hood wrote a long article with the title 'Talented Kleptomania', arguing that Ekman's one skill was to steal ideas from other films and then put them together in one script and pretend it was his. He compared *Meeting in the Night* with Fritz Lang's *The Woman in the Window* (1944), in which Ekman had found the idea for the ending, and then went through most of Ekman's films, tearing them apart. Ekman in turn replied, arguing that what he was doing was only how writers work: they borrow, steal and copy from each other and from themselves, and creating a completely original work is almost impossible. To this Hood replied that Ekman most certainly was not a writer, but just a 'bartender', someone who did not create something unique but took inspirations from others and mixed it all together, albeit a gifted one (Forslund 1982: 179–180). What is interesting to note here is that Robin Hood had often written positive reviews of Ekman's films, as has been stated earlier, so this attack must have come as a surprise. Incidentally, one of the first scripts Ekman wrote in early 1940, for the Bauman-directed film *A Man in Full,* was with Hood (under his real name Bengt Idestam-Almquist), but only Ekman received a screen credit. But regardless of Hood's motives for his attack, Ekman started to doubt himself, even to the point where he was reluctant to go out (Ekman 1955: 186). It is ironic that ten years after *Meeting in the Night* Fritz Lang made *Beyond a Reasonable Doubt* (1956), a film which has almost exactly the same story as Ekman's film. But the ending is very different.

These two films, *Waiting Room for Death* and *Meeting in the Night*, were films that Ekman never wanted to make and never felt comfortable with, but he made them out of obligation to Marmstedt, and to pay the bills. It would therefore be tempting to see the script he wrote for *Love and Downhill Racing* as a comment on these troubles of early 1946. However, even though *Love and Downhill Racing* was released in 1946, it was actually made in the spring of 1944, and it was more a coincidence that its appearance was so timely. Rather, *Love and Downhill Racing* can be seen as a comment on one of the films Ekman had written in 1943, *Life or Death* (which was discussed in the previous chapter), a film he was unhappy about (Ekman 1955: 158). To be specific, he first wrote a film script in 1943 that he did not want to write, and the next year he wrote a film about a writer who had to write a film script he did not want to write. The first film, *Life and Death,* is about alpine riflemen battling snow and enemy agents and experiencing love in the far north, so already in the title of the second film, *Love and Downhill Racing*, Ekman was making fun of the first one, and they more or less share the same setting. This is yet another example of how self-conscious Ekman's script for *Love and Downhill Racing* is. It was typical of him to work like this.

For his third film as writer-director in 1946 he made one for himself, about people he knew, and called it *While the Door Was Locked*. He wrote it together with Walter Ljungquist, their fourth collaboration, and it is what is now sometimes called a 'multi-protagonist film', in that it has no main character, but follows the lives of several separate characters. The setting is an apartment building in Stockholm where during one evening and the following night the lives of the people who live in the various apartments are sketched out for the viewer. Among the people who figure in the film are the caretaker, a prostitute, an ageing theatre actress, a playboy officer and an unhappily married couple. The film could therefore be seen as the second instalment of the unofficial *folkhem* trilogy, in between *Common People* and *We Three Debutantes*.

As in *Wandering with the Moon*, these characters can be seen as spokespersons for characteristic themes and preoccupations of Ekman's. One clear example of this is a discussion between a man and a woman on the verge of divorce. The wife says that she wants to meet new people who are 'interesting, not narrow-minded and petty'. The husband responds: 'You mean like me?' And the wife replies: 'No, of course not, but like Swedes in general, sitting here, content and smug, isolated from the outside world'. Here she is in good company with all those Ekman characters that are tired of conformity and long for other lives, other worlds. She does not say, like so many others have done in Ekman's films, that she would like to go to South America, but she might as well have done so.

Another telling example is a monologue, more or less, by an old diplomat, who used to live in Paris but is now retired in Stockholm. He is at one point standing outside the building with the caretaker, Johansson, and says to him: 'One should live while one is young, Johansson, and have fun. But God only knows that it is not easy in our so-called *folkhem*'; to which Johansson replies: 'No, it's not so damn funny, that's for sure'. The old diplomat continues: 'No, it is not. We think that we live in a free country but nothing could be further from the truth. We all have our probation officers and walk around being discontent, but do we protest? No. In a country like France people made a revolution[;] we are satisfied with nagging and writing letters to the newspapers'. Johansson objects and says: 'But we, the little people, have at least become better off', to which the diplomat sighs and says: 'Yes, better perhaps, but more boring, more boring'. The sentiments and arguments expressed by the diplomat can be seen, as has been shown, in almost all of Ekman's films. It is reasonable to suggest that Ekman felt them himself, that they were his own personal beliefs. This will be elaborated in later chapters.

But Ekman plays an intricate double game in *While the Door Was Locked*. It opens with a shot of a city at dusk, with Ekman's voice telling the audience where the film is set and what it is about, and then introducing the first person who appears in the shot, as the camera has zoomed in on a building. Ekman is also acting in the film, but the Ekman speaking is Ekman the filmmaker, not the character Ekman is playing in the film. This is an example of how with internal auteurs, such as Ekman, there is a risk of forgetting to separate the filmmaker from the actor and from the character. But since it is Ekman the filmmaker who is doing the voice-over in *While the Door Was Locked* and not the character he is playing, there is an implicit suggestion that these two are not the same. The filmmaker and the character are two different entities, and should not be confused.

The film is also something of a tour de force in editing and storytelling. It begins with a tour of the building where the camera just follows one character after another to introduce them. It is a sort of 'relay race narrative', as one character hands over the camera, in a manner of speaking, to the next, and then to the next, until everybody has been introduced and been given a brief sketch of who they are. The economy with which this is done can be illustrated with the case of the ageing theatre actress. The caretaker and his wife are talking about her, saying that she does not get any parts to play any more, nor does she have any servants any more, and the wife says: 'And it's not hard to guess why'. Then there is a cut to the actress pouring herself a drink and toasting her reflection in the mirror, the cut suggesting that the reason she is in decline is because she has become an alcoholic.

The censors were not impressed by this, especially in view of the film's sympathetic portrait of a prostitute, and demanded several cuts a week before the official premiere. After Ekman had re-edited the film, the censors gave it the green light (Forslund 1982: 181–182). It opened on Boxing Day 1946, one month after they had finished filming. As far as the critics were concerned this was one of Ekman's best films. They wrote that it was as good as any Swedish film could be and, as they often did, compared it to international, especially French, cinema. Many critics noticed that Ekman had apparently based his characters on real-life people. Robin Hood wrote, in reference to his former critique of Ekman, that this time Ekman had borrowed not from other films but from real life, and that he had made a brilliant 'miniature portrait of Stockholm' (Hood 1946, trans.).

Again, it is worth pointing out how remarkably productive Ekman was during these years, so it will come as something of a surprise that, in 1947, only one film emerged. *One Swallow Does Not Make a Summer* (*En fluga gör ingen sommar*, 1947), which Ekman wrote, directed, produced and starred in, is interesting for its reversal of gender roles in the marriage. Ekman plays a writer, Bertil Brantemo, struggling with his first novel, and his wife, Inga Brantemo, played by Ekman's wife Eva Henning, is working full-time as a secretary. When the film begins he, in an apron, is preparing dinner and setting the table, while she is delayed at work. It is also pointed out that when they married, contrary to the conventional practice, he took her family name. This arrangement seems to bear out Ekman's feminist credentials. *One Swallow Does Not Make a Summer* is primarily a comedy and Ekman's talent for using innuendo and objects as telling details is much in evidence. The best example comes towards the end of the film. Bertil is having a fling with the daughter of his editor, whereas his wife is on a business trip in Italy and whilst there she is being seduced by her boss. Ekman does not show the audience exactly what happens, but afterwards the locations of a robe, a belt and a tie (they are all in the wrong places), indicate that they both – he at home, and she in Italy – have succumbed to their seducers. Regardless of what happened, it is very delicately handled. Such scenes also contribute to make this the film that most clearly shows Ernst Lubitsch's influence on Ekman, together with the earlier *Happiness Approaches*. What is often referred to as 'the Lubitsch touch' is often noticeable in Ekman's films too, especially the elaborate uses of props, doors and innuendos to suggest rather than spell out what is happening and/ or what the meaning of a particular scene is. Lubitsch and Ekman also have something else in common: they make films about characters who are revolting against, or trying to escape from, society's conventions and the life of the petite bourgeoisie.[5]

Another point of interest is that the film features an ongoing discussion about art and artists. As mentioned earlier, a popular group in Swedish literature during the 1940s was 'Generation 40', and they figure in the film, thinly disguised, with Gunnar Björnstrand playing a writer who is clearly meant to be a member of this group of poets. Ekman's character, Bertil, is trying to write in that style, which leads to an ongoing discussion of their views on life and art. The woman whom Bertil falls for (the daughter of his editor, played by Sonja Wigert) tells him that 'existential pessimism is no longer valid' and that modern writers are engaging in 'unhealthy analysing of psychological complexes'. She is also an artist, a painter, and she complains about feeling inadequate: 'things come too easy for me; whatever I do will not go further than the talented sketch'.

This is one example of how Ekman wrote different characters debating issues with which he himself was struggling. It has sometimes been said by critics that he never went deep enough, that often he seemed to be in a hurry. Furhammar has suggested that Ekman 'could compromise with the wish for perfection and settle for the next best thing' (Furhammar & Åhlund 1993: 89, trans.). In his own writings, books and articles, as well as in interviews, this is something Ekman often comes back to: how he is filled with doubt about his artistry. By writing it into his scripts, his films, he seems to be trying to pre-empt the critics, but also to process his insecurities. Whether or not it is a conscious decision may not be relevant, but it is still noteworthy. The artist's fear that nothing will 'go further than the talented sketch' could have been taken from interviews with Ekman. But there was no need for these doubts. On the contrary, it is the quality of the films that is remarkable. What is more, the constant rediscovery of his films seems to suggest that Ekman was better than he gave himself credit for and even though he was occasionally criticised, the majority of films Ekman made were highly regarded by the critics, won awards and drew large crowds. And despite Ekman's self-doubts the critics found *One Swallow Does Not Make a Summer* funny and amusing.

For his next film, *To Each His Own* (*Var sin väg*, 1948), Ekman returned to one of his most common themes, a couple torn apart because one is an artist and the other is not. It is the same set-up as in *One Swallow Does Not Make a Summer* but this time the man has a traditional job while the woman is an artist, in this case a theatre actress. The film is also a much darker and more anguished work than *One Swallow Does Not Make a Summer*. Both husband and wife are dedicated professionals but she has decided to give up her theatre career and stay with her husband, who is a young, promising and ambitious doctor. But she cannot let go of her theatre dreams, and eventually they are no longer able to compromise. They have an argument and he complains bitterly about her theatre work to which she responds: 'You forget one thing. I love you'. He responds, 'More than the theatre?' – a question which she is unable to answer. They go their different ways, pursuing their respective careers. This is by now familiar Ekman territory: marriage strife and the power of the theatre. Another typical Ekman motif is introduced in a party scene, full of anxiety and awkwardness, where people are talking about South America. One character says: 'Argentina, how lovely it sounds. I've always wanted to go to South America'.

An interesting aspect of *To Each His Own* is its attempt, following *Flames in the Dark*, to explore the workings of a psychotic and cruel character. This time it is a brilliant surgeon, who is also the head of a hospital, and who will be the young doctor's boss. What is unusual here is the film's reluctance to provide easy psychological answers as to why the surgeon behaves as he does. It even plays with the common Freudian explanations that were popular at the time. In a scene towards the end of the film the surgeon is apparently caught off guard, and reveals a frightening childhood memory. He has also said that his wife killed herself. Yet at the very end of the film it is revealed that his wife did not kill herself. She only divorced him and she is still alive. The childhood memory he related cannot be true either. So the audience is none the wiser. There is a double act going on here, with the surgeon playing on the popular Freudian explanations he knows his peers are familiar with, and Ekman doing the same thing with his audience, playing with simplistic ideas as to what causes human behaviour.

The film offers several examples of Ekman's skill of suggesting things visually rather than saying them explicitly. The most powerful moment is when Ekman lets the audience know that the couple have separated. In one scene the husband, alone at home, receives a letter and in the next shot the wife's bed is taken upstairs, to the storage room. There is no dialogue, and the content of the letter is not revealed; only the removal of the bed signifies what the letter was about.

The ending of *To Each His Own* is something of a surprise, in that the wife returns to her husband and says that she will give up the theatre in order to save their relationship. This might be the only time this happens in an Ekman film, that love for a person is stronger than love of a vocation. It may also feel like something of a disappointment that it is the woman who gives up her professional career and not the man; in general in Ekman's films the women are the stronger characters, and it is almost always they who have the last laugh or the final say. In the 1950s Ekman went on to make even more powerful films about the relationship between men and women, in which he criticised male hypocrisy and chauvinism.

Ekman had made these last four films for the production company Europa Film, with which he had signed a two-year contract. That contract now came to an end, and he returned to Terra and his long-time producer partner Lorens Marmstedt. The first film they made together was a sequel to their financially most successful film, *Little Märta Steps Forward*, called *The Return of Little Märta* (*Lilla Märta kommer tillbaka*, 1948). In the title sequence of the film Ekman is credited with thirteen different roles, from head of production and director to composer and actor, which says a lot about his creativity. The film is a mildly amusing, farcical comedy set on a farm in the countryside during the Second World War. It is also, somewhat unexpectedly, a satire of the Nazis. Ekman and Stig Järrel play the lead characters, who discover an implausible network of Nazi spies in the middle of nowhere. What is interesting is that rather than having an obvious ending, as such, the film just stops, all of a sudden, in the middle of a chase scene. It is as if Ekman neither knew nor cared how it should end, and just walked away from it.

But there would be no traces of farcical comedy in his next film, *The Banquet* (*Banketten*, 1948). This would be one of his most celebrated and groundbreaking works, and was premiered at Christmas. Even if Ekman had made dark and serious work before 1948, *The Banquet* must still be considered a step further in mood, in that it is a piercing and chilling film. The setting is an upper-class area in Stockholm and the film is about a wealthy family, consisting of a mother, a father, two sons and a daughter. The first scene is a travelling shot along one of Stockholm's most fashionable streets. The camera eventually focuses on a particular window, which is being opened by a maid to feed some birds. In that apartment lives the mother, the father and the youngest son, and it is here and in the married daughter's apartment that most of the film will take place. The story covers a few days before a big banquet held in honour of the father, a rich banker. He is retiring, and he would like someone to take over the business after him, but there are no suitable candidates. The father resents the older son, the son-in-law is not suitable, the daughter is of the wrong sex and the youngest son has no interest in following in his father's footsteps – especially not since he, the son, is a committed communist, and is renouncing the family's wealth and money. His dream is to go to South America.

That is one of the two main storylines in the film. The other is the relationship between the daughter, Vica, and her husband Hugo. They are played by Eva Henning and Hasse Ekman and their relationship is one of cruelty, jealousy, hatred and masochism. The scenes in their apartment, with their constant outbursts of vitriol and violence, are among the visually most striking in Ekman's career, with the play of light and shadow and the use of interior framing creating elaborate patterns of concealment, imprisonment and claustrophobia. Ekman was for the second time working with the cinematographer Gösta Roosling but instead of the open-air lyricism of *Wandering with The Moon* it often looks more like an American film noir, something shot by the cinematographer John F. Seitz (who worked on *Double Indemnity* (Billy Wilder, 1944) and many other distinguished films).

The Banquet divides its sympathies between the father, the honest businessman from a previous generation who does not understand the modern world, and the youngest son, the communist, who is torn between his hatred of capitalism and his love for his father. Eventually their two lives are incompatible, as are the lives of the daughter and her husband, and slowly the family falls apart. The film ends, much as it begun, with a long travelling shot. Only this time it starts at the window and tracks down the fashionable street, away from the stifling life in the apartment and out into the fresh air of the larger world. The film, although unusually dark, contains several of Ekman's motifs, including the wish to move to South America. What is new is that the only loving relationship is between a son and his father. It is one of the bitter tragedies of the film that not even this love will be enough. The son has to leave, as his freedom is more important to him than family and traditions.

The Banquet is one of Ekman's most interior films, both because it is about the inner lives of the characters and because it is almost exclusively shot indoors. The setting could be almost anywhere in the world. The setting is not even important for the film. With the exception of *Love and Downhill Racing*, which is set in the far north of Sweden and takes advantage of that setting, none of the films mentioned in this chapter has a particularly Swedish setting, in terms of geography and topography. They could be set anywhere. But in terms of characters and sensibilities they have a strong connection with Swedish culture at the time, and *While the Door Was Locked* in particular is about the people of Stockholm. It can be seen as a discussion of the lives of urban Swedes in a post-war context. Films such as *One Swallow Does Not Make a Summer* and *To Each His Own* (which would constitute an interesting double feature) can also be seen as snapshots of what it was like to live in Sweden in 1947–1948. The films do not say anything about the nation as a whole, but implicitly, through the characters' behaviour and experiences, the audience will get a sense of Swedish life.

If Ekman for some time had been seen as 'the best' by the Swedish film critics, now, by the end of the 1940s, the rivalry with Bergman would become a key aspect of both their careers for several years and it would take its toll on them, especially on Ekman. Bergman had begun working as a director of a children's theatre in the centre of Stockholm in 1942, where he showed that besides being a talented director, he also was an astute businessman with a good sense of publicity. This would continue to serve him well after he became a filmmaker. His first film script was *Torment*, which he sent to SF in 1943. After many alterations, including those suggested by the director Alf Sjöberg, it was made into a film in 1944, becoming one of the most popular Swedish films of the 1940s. Two years after *Torment* Bergman directed his first film, *Crisis* (*Kris*, 1946), which was followed by almost two films each year for the rest of the 1940s. He also worked simultaneously as a theatre director in first Helsingborg and then Göteborg, two cities in the south-west of Sweden.

The films Bergman made in the 1940s were varied in style, and he has said that he was influenced by, among others, Roberto Rossellini and Michael Curtiz (Björkman et al. 1993). As alluded to earlier, the French poetic-realist films of Marcel Carné and Jacques Prévert were another influence, most clearly seen in *A Ship to India* (*Skepp till Indialand*, 1947). It was not until 1949 with *Prison* aka *The Devil's Wanton* (*Fängelse*) that Bergman made a film which made a lasting impression. *Prison* is also one of three films that Bergman made using Ekman as a key actor. The other two are *Thirst* aka *Three Strange Loves* (*Törst*, 1949) and *Sawdust and Tinsel*. The third provided Ekman's biggest part, as a handsome but devilish actor who seduces a married woman, played by Harriet Andersson, and then taunts her husband with his conquest.

Early on there was rivalry between Ekman and Bergman, possibly because they were considered the two best filmmakers by the critics. The first time a reference was made to a Bergman film when one of Ekman's was reviewed was in 1945, when *Wandering with the Moon* was called the 'most promising film since Torment' (Pavane 1945, trans.) in *BLM*. On the other hand, in 1950 a critic wrote that 'in the perpetual dialogue between Ingmar Bergman and Hasse Ekman' he preferred to listen to Ekman (Björkman 1950, trans.). When Ekman made *Royal Rabble* this constant comparison had not really begun, but even so the line that was quoted above, 'Why do you have to compare? I think it is silly', is given additional resonance. It should be remembered, however, that they also shared many things and Bergman worked with Ekman's producer, Lorens Marmstedt, for two years, making three films. They were not enemies, only two independent and competitive filmmakers, even if the rivalry was what was mostly said in public, and what is mostly remembered today. In an interview Bergman commented on this, saying that on the one hand Ekman had been a big support, especially after Bergman was severely criticised for *A Ship to India*, but he was also envious of Ekman's calm professionalism and angry about the times when Ekman got to see the dailies of Bergman's *Thirst*, because the producer did not trust Bergman (Furhammar & Åhlund 1993: 3–7). Ekman, on the other hand, said that he was sometimes jealous of Bergman's successes, but that he felt that the successes were deserved (Ekman 1955: 225). Furhammar has written that in some ways the competition between Bergman and Ekman was 'childish' but at the same time he argues that: 'the seriousness of the struggle cannot be questioned, even if neither Ekman nor Bergman admitted any hostility towards each other' (Furhammar 1991: 231–232, trans.).

As mentioned, Bergman's *Prison* was a substantial critical success. It tells two stories, one about three friends (a filmmaker, played by Ekman, a journalist, played by Birger Malmsten, and the woman they both love, played by Eva Henning) and one about a young girl, played by Doris Svedlund, who is forced to become a prostitute, has her newborn baby stolen and eventually commits suicide. The connection between the two stories is that the journalist appears in both, as he is telling his friends the story about the prostitute in one, and in the other tries to 'save' her. The film begins with a man saying that the devil rules the world, and ends with the comment that since there is no God, there is no hope. In *Prison* Bergman arguably makes the case that we are either tortured souls to be pitied or cruel animals to be loathed.

One consequence of *Prison* was that it prompted Ekman to make, as he himself called it, an 'anti-Bergman film' (Malgefors: 1961): *The Girl from the Third Row* (*Flickan från tredje raden*, 1949). *The Girl from the Third Row* begins with the last act of a play. The play ends with the only character on stage committing suicide. The curtains then fall and the camera travels among the audience, listening to some of their comments. They all hate it, and someone says that maybe the director should stick to farce and comedies instead. The actor, who also wrote and directed the play, and owns the theatre, is played by Ekman, who of course also wrote, directed and produced the film. After the audience has left and the theatre is deserted, Sture Anker, Ekman's character, sits alone and smokes a cigarette, until he gets up and walks out on stage, making a cynical comment to himself about his own fiasco. Then a woman appears out of the shadows, saying that she will tell him a story about life, since he apparently knows so little about it (see figure 4.3). The story concerns a golden ring and the people whose lives are affected by it. Reluctantly, he listens to it, while building a house of cards, and the film then moves back and forth between the characters on the stage, and the story she is telling. That story is set in several parts of Stockholm, among the rich as well as the poor, among happy and distressed, loving and hateful individuals, and together these individuals create a picture of humanity in all its complexity. There are no heroes and no devils; there are just humans with their capacity for cruelty and compassion. In one of the episodes, two poor parents are forced to give up their daughter for adoption; in another a woman leaves her husband for her lover. In a third episode, an accountant is exposed as an embezzler by his employer. In these three episodes of the story, and in some of the others as well, through chance or the kindness of strangers eventually things work out, and some kind of equilibrium is reached. Things will not be perfect, but there will still be reasons to be hopeful.

Both *Prison* and *The Girl from the Third Row* have unusual narrative structures, and there are structural similarities. Both have a prologue, which is set in a

Figure 4.3: Sture Anker (Hasse Ekman) and the girl from the third row (Eva Henning) in *The Girl from the Third Row*. Photo courtesy of Studio S Entertainment. Image from the Swedish Film Institute Archives.

backstage milieu, in Bergman's case a film set; in Ekman's a theatre. This setting is used as a framing device for the main narrative, which in Bergman's case is that of the world as hell, and in Ekman's that of a world of both hope and despair. Another shared device is to have the internal story narrated by an all-knowing character, telling the other characters, and the audience, their story. Thus this character in a way becomes the filmmaker, or at least a spokesperson for the filmmaker. In Bergman's case it is the journalist, and in Ekman's it is the mysterious woman, the girl from the third row. Yet another similarity is of course that the character to whom the story is narrated is played by Hasse Ekman in both cases. Here the intertextuality becomes increasingly complex because in Bergman's film, Ekman is in a way playing himself, as he is seen by Bergman and the public, whereas in Ekman's film, Ekman is in a way playing Bergman, as he is seen by Ekman and the public. In an article from 1995, Cecilia Axelsson argues that by giving this part to Ekman, Bergman was deliberately trying to further his own career, by portraying himself, Bergman, as the artist, and portraying Ekman as the studio hack (Axelsson 1995). It is questionable how cunning Bergman's motives really were, but it is possible that he was thinking along those lines.

The critics liked both of the films, but with Bergman's they were more impressed by the style and form than they were by the stories told. It was criticised for being forced, pathetic and overtly symbolic, whereas Ekman's was criticised for being occasionally naïve and too generous. Although the critics did not know at the time of reviewing it that Ekman was specifically aiming his film at Bergman, they still understood its intentions. One wrote: '[Ekman] has constructed a film which, consciously or unconsciously, aims at Sartre, but hits Ingmar Bergman' (A.G.B. 1949, trans.), and another wrote that it felt like 'Ekman in this film dared to attack Bergman at close range' (Björkman 1949, trans.). In an interview a few years later Ekman said that Bergman 'had the appearance of being the spokesperson for Generation 40 in Swedish cinema. My film wanted to be a reaction against this fashionable stance of talking about everything's meaninglessness' (Malgefors 1961, trans.).

This is yet another instance where the connections between Bergman and Generation 40 can be seen. Ekman had playfully parodied this group and Bergman too when making *One Swallow Does Not Make a Summer*, but *The Girl from the Third Row* was Ekman's most decisive and complete rebuttal of this worldview. His argument in the film seems to be that although cruelty, betrayal, despair and death exist, that is only half of the story. Love, beauty, trust and kindness also exist, and the former do not negate the latter. To say that the world is hell is just a shallow pose. It is a complex world and we are all torn, just as in *Changing Trains*, where the very narrative construction of the film has the audience moving back and forth between hope and despair, love and betrayal, life and death. Here Ekman's focus on acting, playing parts and hiding our identities comes into play again. If we live behind a mask maybe our lives and the lives of others become more bearable, at least for a while. In many respects the film is a companion piece to *Wandering with the Moon*, which also has a number of different characters all acting out different aspects of humanity and life, and balancing precariously between happiness and despair. And as with *Wandering with the Moon*, it is again appropriate to mention Jean Renoir as a reference point, and another French filmmaker, Julien Duvivier. Duvivier was one of the major filmmakers in France before the Second World War, together with Renoir and Carné, and one point of reference is Duvivier's film *Christine* (*Un carnet de bal*, 1937), which is about a woman who after her husband dies re-evaluates her life and visits all those men she once knew but did not marry, to see what has become of them. It has the same episodic structure as some of Ekman's best films. Duvivier later remade *Christine* in the US with the title *Lydia* (1941). The following year Duvivier made *Tales of Manhattan* (1942). As it is the story of a tailcoat that moves from one owner to another, there is a similarity with the structure of *The Girl from the Third Row*, with one ring going from one owner to another.

One of the characters in *The Girl from the Third Row* is a painter, and as has been observed already, Ekman's use of painters and paintings is a recurring motif. In one episode an easy-going husband meets, without realising it, his wife's lover. The husband does not know about the affair, but the lover knows about the husband. The lover is also a painter, of abstract art, and they are discussing one of his paintings. The husband does not understand the painting, which exemplifies all that is wrong with him, as far as his wife is concerned, and what is wrong with their marriage. The marriage, although safe and secure, is also boring, lacking in adventure and imagination, and is suffocating her, whereas the artist holds the promise of a completely different life. In the film the husband comes across as something of a buffoon, yet very sweet and kind, and it seems that if he had understood the painting he might still be with his wife.

The reasons for describing this as an 'anti-Bergman' film are plentiful. First of all, the character Ekman is playing, Sture Anker, is too close to the popular view of Bergman for the resemblance to go unnoticed. But the film should not be read as a parody of Bergman. Sture Anker is being taught a lesson in the film, but he is not being ridiculed. Rather, he is treated with a combination of respect and pity and at the end he has become a better person. He has learnt his lesson. Second, the film's debate between Sture Anker and the girl touches upon many subjects that were fashionable at the time, including nihilism and existentialism, which is why some critics mentioned Jean-Paul Sartre in their reviews. Some characters and scenes in the film are also similar to characters and scenes in films of other filmmakers, such as Bergman, but here a new twist is given to these characters and scenes. It is not only Bergman, but the whole of Generation 40, that would have recognised particular lines of dialogue and even the setting of the film. In addition, the staging of the play that opens the film was copied from a performance of Sartre's play *No Exit* (*Huis clos*) from 1944 at the Royal Dramatic Theatre. For the audience at the time it was clear what Ekman was reacting against, and as Bergman was arguably a central person in the movement Ekman was engaging with, calling it an 'anti-Bergman' film made perfect sense. This would not be the last time Ekman and Bergman were engaged in these kinds of games. But whereas future instances would be more humorous, more like parody, in *The Girl from the Third Row* it is on a deeper level.

The competition between Ekman and Bergman was reflected in the critics' seasonal votes for best Swedish films. In 1946–1947 Bergman won with *It Rains on Our Love* and Ekman's *While the Door Was Locked* came second. For the next few years one of the two would always win, and the other came in second or third. In 1949–1950 *The Girl from the Third Row* came in fourth. In second place was Sjöberg's *Only a Mother* and in third place was Bergman's *Thirst*. But the film that won that season was another film by Ekman, *Girl with Hyacinths*. That film will occupy a large part of the next chapter.

Notes

1. Garson Kanin is today best known for having written several films for George Cukor, such as *Adam's Rib* (1949) with Judy Holliday, Katherine Hepburn and Spender Tracy and *Born Yesterday* (1950) with Judy Holliday and William Holden. But he also directed a number of films in the late 1930s and early 1940s such as *Bachelor Mother* (1939) and *Tom, Dick and Harry* (1941), both with Ginger Rogers.
2. Translating military ranks from Swedish to English is not straightforward, but a British 'sub-lieutenant' should be the equivalent to a Swedish fänrik.

3.　According to Ekman, Dagmar Edqvist was approached to make the script more psychologically truthful. This was because 'she had once been secretary to a professor of psychiatry' (Ekman 1955: 145, trans.).

4.　Gabin and Morgan acted together as a doomed couple in *Port of Shadows* (*Quai de brumes* 1938), under the direction of Marcel Carné. Interestingly, in his book *Images: My Life in Film* (1994: 132), Ingmar Bergman writes than in 1946, when he made *It Rains on Our Love* (*Det regnar på vår kärlek*) for Lorens Marmstedt, he too was scolded by Marmstedt for trying to be Carné and his lead actor for trying to be Jean Gabin.

5.　There are many books about Lubitsch but see, for example, Poague (1978) and Eyman (1993).

CHAPTER 5

The Early 1950s

The end of the 1940s saw Hasse Ekman and Ingmar Bergman locked in competition, and Ekman was alternating between making personal films and making films to honour commitments. Ekman's output in the 1950s would primarily concern itself with intimate and personal films, at least until 1956. That year saw both the emergence of television and a change in Ekman's relationship with Bergman and his view of himself as a filmmaker. This chapter will cover the years 1950 to 1956. It begins, however, with a discussion of Ekman's theatre works.

A topic that has not been elaborated upon yet is Ekman's work as a stage director. He had earlier in his career directed for the theatre, but did so more frequently from 1950. That year Intima Teatern (The Intimate Theatre)[1] opened in Stockholm, under the management of Lorens Marmstedt, and it would soon be known as the 'Ekman Theatre' because Ekman had a string of successes there, both as an actor and as a director. Very little has been written about his stage career, and since it is impossible to rewatch the plays and the performances it is sadly beyond the scope and ability of this book to discuss his theatre work in any depth, beyond pointing out that his role in Swedish theatre was important. Here too there was competition with Bergman. The first three plays that opened on Intima Teatern were directed by Bergman but none of them was successful, commercially. Then Ekman took over, directing Elmer Rice's play *Dream Girl*, which ran successfully for two seasons (Forslund 1982: 196). In total he directed more than twenty plays, including those written by him and plays by writers such as Robert E. Sherwood and Peter Shaffer. He also brought Reginald Rose's play *Twelve Angry Men* to the Swedish stage for the first time. It is worth noting here that in 1951–1952 Ekman directed Jean Anouilh's play *The Traveller without Luggage* (*Le voyageur sans bagage*) (ibid.: 198). With its story of lost identities, and people assuming the identities of others, it must have seemed a perfect fit for Ekman. Besides directing, he was also in constant demand as an actor. Yet it should be said that whereas Alf Sjöberg and Ingmar Bergman had theatre careers that were equal in importance to their film careers, and in Sjöberg's case the theatre was arguably more important than the cinema, this was not the case with Ekman. In his autobiography *Den vackra ankungen* he barely mentions his theatre work at all and focuses almost entirely on his personal life and his work as a film-maker. To what extent his experience of directing films influenced his work on the stage, and vice versa, is not possible to say without having seen the stage work.

Besides working at the theatre, in 1950 Ekman also made three films. They are among his most interesting. As has been made clear, he occasionally made films that drew on his own personal experiences and sometimes used intricate flash-back structures to tell his stories. He would do both in *Girl with Hyacinths*, his first film of the new decade. It begins with a woman, Dagmar Brink, committing sui-cide, and then tells the story of who she was and how she came to take her life. The truth, however, always remains elusive, and the core of the main character is somehow out of reach. There are similarities between the narrative structure of *Girl with Hyacinths* and that of Ekman's earlier film *Changing Trains*, the differ-ences being that the dying woman is narrating the story in *Changing Trains* but in *Girl with Hyacinths* it is the dead woman's neighbours who are investigating her death. The flashbacks in *Girl with Hyacinths* are not chronological, in the sense that the second flashback reveals something that happened before the events shown in the first flashback, and the third flashback tells of something that hap-pened chronologically between the events in the first and second flashbacks, and so on, which makes the film deserving of additional viewings. Those who have written about *Girl with Hyacinths* before have all mentioned Welles's *Citizen Kane* as an inspiration for the structure. It is easy to see why as both films begin with the death of the main character and then the rest of the film is an investigation of a mystery surrounding the death, told in non-chronological flashbacks. Ekman has himself also acknowledged that he was inspired by Welles (Åhlund & Carlsson 1993). However, the two films are different and the resemblance is only in the structure. These differences are revealing, however, for what they say about each filmmaker. *Citizen Kane* is about a man who wants to conquer the world; *Girl with Hyacinths* is about a woman who wants to hide from it. *Citizen Kane* is about a man who is consumed by his own ego; *Girl with Hyacinths* is about a woman consumed by the world. *Citizen Kane* is about a so-called 'great man' who was larger than life; Ekman's film is about an ordinary girl. It is one of Ekman's strengths that he tells stories about the lives of ordinary people and yet makes these stories interesting, important and deeply moving.

Ekman has said that the inspiration for the script came from a relative of his then-wife Eva Henning, who plays the main character, Dagmar Brink. He has also said that the three men in Dagmar's life can be seen as various aspects of his own persona. As he writes in his autobiography (referring to himself in third person):

> *He himself is split between three male characters in the film: 1. the on the one hand decent and bourgeois, but at the same time despotic and jealous, hus-band who had neither the capacity nor the need to understand his wife, 2. the ruthless, self-absorbed, work-obsessed painter who felt her bourgeois traits as stifling and had neither the time nor the inclination to understand, 3. the pre-sumptuous [and] shallow but unremarkable gramophone singer who thought he understood, but did not understand anything. Each and every one repre-sented different aspects of the writer. (Ekman 1955: 201–202, trans. emphasis in the original)*

For a change Ekman himself did not play a part in the film, and this might have been because there was no role for him, having split himself up into three parts. Forslund also suggests that the neighbour/writer who conducts the investigation probably had something of Ekman written into the part as well. To this, Bengt Forslund has added that the character Elias Körner, a painter played by Anders Ek (see figure 5.1), has a resemblance to the then recently deceased painter Curt Clemens (Forslund 1982: 190).

One striking thing about the film is its sensitive subjects. Suicide was in itself such a sensitive topic, but even more sensitive was the fact that the girl in *Girl with Hyacinths* is a lesbian: this is the hidden truth. Homosexuality was at this time definitely not a mainstream subject, neither in films nor in society as a whole. Homosexuality had been decriminalised as recently as 1944, but it was still not talked about, so the film led to much debate. The debate seems not to have been alarmist or critical, but rather a serious attempt to discuss issues which had been taboo before. Ekman was open about this, and he participated in the debate. He said in an interview that he thought that 'the day will come when this phenom-enon is no longer considered ugly and dirty' and: 'If *Girl with Hyacinths* in some way can contribute to clear the air around the debate about homosexuals the work has not been in vain' (Heed 1950, trans.).[2]

The film came out after the Kinsey Report had been translated into Swedish and the first part, *Sexual Behaviour in the Human Male*, published in 1949 (Bergenheim 2009: 128). *Sexual Behaviour in the Human Female* appeared a few years later. The Kinsey Report was an investigation into the sexual life of US

Figure 5.1: Elias Körner (Anders Ek) and Anders Wikner (Ulf Palme) with the painting of Dagmar Brink in *Girl with Hyacinths*. Photo courtesy of Studio S Entertainment. Image from the Swedish Film Institute Archives.

Americans, both male and female. Alfred Kinsey and his colleagues argued that homosexuality was common, and just as 'natural' as heterosexuality, and that it was not really correct or helpful to define people based on their sexuality, since sexuality was not something stable, but fluctuating. In 1950, the same year as *Girl with Hyacinths* was released, a Swedish lobby group for gay, lesbian and bisexual people was founded, called RFSL (Riksförbundet för Sexuellt Likaberättigande, the National Society for Sexual Equality). Interestingly, and as a sign of how unaware the population was of the very existence of homosexuality, or at least how reluctant society was to admit to it, a survey conducted by one of Sweden's biggest newspapers, *Aftonbladet*, revealed that only 60 per cent of the audience understood the context and meaning of the film. A psychologist tried to explain this by calling homosexuality a cultural 'blind spot' (Heed 1950, trans.).

One probable reason for this, and what is also so remarkable about *Girl with Hyacinths*, is that Dagmar Brink is a perfectly 'normal' woman; she does not stand out, nor has she any characteristics that the audience would have found strange or unsettling. By contrast, in Bergman's *Thirst* there is a lesbian character, but she is an aggressive, predatory woman, and the main character avoids her. Dagmar Brink, on the other hand, is no different from any other female character in Ekman's films. The fact that she is a lesbian is in one sense not important, especially since it is not even apparent in the film. It is true that she commits suicide, but not *because* she is a homosexual, or because she is sickened by her own feelings; it is because her one true love has betrayed her. With her melancholy disposition she would in all likelihood have committed suicide had she been heterosexual too, if she had been betrayed. The film is not really about homosexuality either, but more about women in general, one of whom happens to be lesbian, and in this sense it is clearly a feminist film. There is a sense of female rapport, of support and shared common grounds, of a female community that the men do not understand and cannot join; a sense that women need to look after each other, as a way of surviving in a male-chauvinistic world. One such example is when, in one of the flashbacks, Dagmar tries to commit suicide the first time (as far as the audience knows), but a female neighbour sees her and interferes. They then sit together and talk about life and suffering and the sequence ends with the neighbour putting Dagmar to bed, and then sitting at Dagmar's bedside, holding her hand, until she falls asleep. In this world of self-righteous men who think they can seduce and exploit women and then just pay them off, without taking any real responsibility, the film shows that there is an alternative, a world of women standing up for each other, and covering each other's backs. In that context it is significant that in the last scene, the man who is investigating Dagmar's suicide has not understood anything. Only his wife knows the truth, but she does not tell him. In this world some things are better kept among the women, in their world of sisterhood, as a protection against the men.

For the perceptive spectator, Ekman has filled the frame with little hints as to the theme of the film, but if they were hard to spot then, they are even more difficult today perhaps, since these are both local and time-bound and might not be recognised by a present-day audience. In Dagmar's apartment there are a few books and a painting that are signifiers of female homosexuality and suicide, such as poetry by Karin Boye and Edith Södergran, and a painting from 1927 by the Swedish painter Sven Xet Erixson called *Flickor på ängen* (*Girls in a Meadow*), with two women decorating each other with flowers. As has been argued earlier, paintings often play a part in Ekman's films and *Girl with Hyacinths* is partly about a painter and a painting that is associated with the main character. The title of the film is the title of a painting which is being painted during the course of the film, a portrait of the main character. This in some way mirrors the whole idea of the film, which is also an attempt to paint a picture, albeit with moving images instead of a still portrait. (The inspiration for the film's title might have been a few lines, about a hyacinth girl, in T.S. Eliot's poem *The Waste Land*.)

Another recurring motif in Ekman's films is characters who keep things hidden, play parts, are pretending or are wanting to be something other than what they are. In a sense Dagmar Brink does this more than any other character in Ekman's films. It is almost what defines her. It also ties in with a poem by Edith Södergran that Dagmar loves. A few lines are spoken in the film and they read thus (in a translation by Martin Allwood): 'All my life I will be the silent one, / the talkers are like the babbling brook which gives itself away; / I will be a lonely tree in the plain'.[3] As the first flashbacks take place before homosexuality was legalised, Dagmar Brink would not have had much of a choice other than to hide her inner thoughts and desires. There are links between her and Inga Dahl in *Changing Trains*, Dan in *Wandering with the Moon* and other Ekman characters, loners and dreamers who have a difficult time in this world.

Stylistically, the film is one of Ekman's most accomplished, and the cinematography by Göran Strindberg is often striking. Ekman had previously made films in such a sombre style, using rain, shadows and stark contrasts between light and dark, especially in *Waiting Room for Death* and *The Banquet*. Ekman and Strindberg would continue to develop this style in *The White Cat* (*Den vita katten*, 1950), discussed later in this chapter. Besides the lighting, *Girl with Hyacinths* has many of Ekman's stylistic trademarks. There are the long takes, imaginative editing and efforts to introduce real-world phenomena, creating images and scenes that in a sense contextualise this film's particular story. One example is when Dagmar Brink's maid comes to her apartment in the morning and opens the window and the sun is reflected in the window glass. This is not necessary for the story, but it is there because the sun was there, or, if it was shot in a studio, because the sun would have been there in real life. Another example is when a little boy on a tricycle comes along the pavement just after the ambulance has arrived to pick up the body of Dagmar. The importance of the boy is that he brings in an element from the outside world, the world beyond the story. This adds poignancy by making the film feel real, but it also makes the unfolding drama less pressing, since for this little boy the suicide and that particular storyline is not important.

He does not even know about it, which suggests that the world is bigger than the individuals in it. Sound is also used to this effect, such as in a sequence in which Dagmar and a man who may be her father are having a tense discussion in his office, while on the soundtrack men are heard shovelling snow outside. The scene when the maid discovers Dagmar's body also exemplifies Ekman's editing skills. After she has opened the window she turns around, sees the body and screams; the camera is close to her face (the audience does not see what she sees). As soon as she begins to scream, Ekman cuts to a poster with the figure of Death with a scythe, hanging on the wall of the police station that the maid has called to report the death of her employer.

There is another subtext to the film. It is yet another film in which Ekman deals with the Second World War, and Nazism. The suicide takes place in 1949, but the flashbacks go back to the war years, and it is clear that Dagmar was fiercely anti-Nazi, whereas others around her do not share her principled objections against them. This is also, partly, a reason why she commits suicide. The film can be seen as an allegorical rejection of Sweden's ambivalent stance during the war, as discussed in chapter 2, with Dagmar playing the part of Sweden's conscience, as it were, or the conscientious objector. This was not something picked up by the critics, but many of them wrote that *Girl with Hyacinths* was Ekman's best film so far (or second best, after *Changing Trains*), with praise for the acting, the dialogue and the fluent storytelling. When the Swedish film critics at the end of the year voted for best Swedish film of the season, *Girl with Hyacinths* won a clear victory, with 113 points.

But for all the praise it received, Ekman was now constantly being reminded of the presence of his rival, Bergman. In an interview during the making of *Girl with Hyacinths* Ekman was asked if he was trying to make a 'Bergman film'. He replied: 'Ingmar Bergman? Well, I would not say that – a girl can commit suicide at the beginning of a film without it having to be an Ingmar Bergman' (Wernlöf 1949, trans.). That question reveals as much about contemporary Swedish cinema as it does about the filmmakers' rivalry, with some critics writing, by way of praising Ekman, that *Girl with Hyacinths* was at least as good as Bergman's work.

Ekman's next film, *Knight of Hearts* (*Hjärter knekt*, 1950), can be seen as an attack on the playboy attitude of which he was accused. This is a cruel and bitter film, but told with exquisite style and verve. It is a complex story which tells of two brothers, Anders and Wilhelm Canitz, from a wealthy, upper-class family. They have chosen two completely different paths. Anders, played by Ekman, spends all his money on women, horses and gambling, whereas Wilhelm is hard-working and diligent. Anders seduces most women he meets, as he is handsome, charming and fun, and among the women with whom he has affairs, one is his sister-in-law. Eventually his irresponsible behaviour and the emptiness of his life catch up with him and he is more or less forced to commit suicide. It is on paper a fairly conventional moral story, somewhat surprisingly so for an Ekman film. But there is more to it than a brief summary can reveal. Take for example a statement made by another woman Anders had an affair with and that his brother also desired. She says to Wilhelm: 'I'm so happy I got three months with him rather than years of petit-bourgeois self-righteousness married to you'. This kind of comment recurs every now and then in Ekman's oeuvre – it is part of his worldview – and this sentiment gives the film an edge, raising it above the conventional morality it might seem to adhere to. The film is ambivalent in its treatment of the characters, and that includes Anders, a man who for all his faults has charm and an appetite for life. But in this film Ekman seems to want to suggest the potential dangers of the kind of lifestyle, free from conventions and society, that he usually celebrates, or rather that his characters habitually dream about. To some extent the film continued the dark subtexts of *Girl with Hyacinths*, and they would become even more dark and troubling in his next film.

The year 1950 was a very productive one for Ekman, and two films written by him opened around Christmas that year: *The White Cat*, which he also directed, on 26 December and *The Kiss on the Cruise* (*Kyssen på kryssen*), which Arne Mattsson directed, on 16 December. *The White Cat* was written and directed by Ekman after a novel by Walter Ljungquist, and is a psychological thriller about a man who has forgotten who he is. So ten years after *With You in My Arms* Ekman returned to the same basic premise, only this time there were few jokes. Instead, *The White Cat* is probably the darkest and cruellest film Ekman ever made, and it still has the potential to shock and disturb. The opening sequence, which is almost without dialogue, shows a man (Alf Kjellin) arriving by train at the central station in Stockholm. He just sits there, staring blankly in front of him, after the train has stopped and all the other passengers have got off. Eventually, he gets up and starts walking around the station, and at one point he tries to leave, but when he sees two policemen he returns and walks up to a café and sits down to have a coffee. He overhears two women reading a newspaper article about an escaped convict, a rapist, and the description seems to be his. The convict is said to have a scar on his face, and the man goes to a mirror to check whether he has one. He does not, and he returns to the café. (In Anouilh's play *The Traveller without Luggage* (mentioned above) there is a similar incident, except that the man finds out that he *does* have a scar when he looks in the mirror.)

This is Ekman's most striking opening sequence, and it is shot by Göran Strindberg in an impressive style with great depth of field and almost expression-istic lighting. Like *Girl with Hyacinths*, the visual style of the film as a whole recalls aspects of film noir, but film noir spiked with surrealism. *The White Cat* has a distinct Freudian theme and is filled with dream imagery, nightmares of often violent and/or sexual content. The man, whose name remains a mystery through-out the film, has lost his memory and is haunted by those nightmares. Unusually for Ekman, the film has several extreme close-ups of faces, deep in fear and full of sweat. The themes of guilt and disorientation also recall American film noir – films such as *The Blue Dahlia* (George Marshall, 1946).

The waitress at the station café (Eva Henning) takes an interest in the man, and when her shift is over they walk together through town to her apartment. She wants them to work together to try to find the key to his mind, memory and iden-tity. He is wary of discovering the truth, since whatever it is, it is not going to be pretty. Maybe his amnesia is 'an escape from a reality that is unbearable', as he says. Eventually, however, he gets to the bottom of his story. It turns out that he was once married but that he found out that his wife had an affair with a painter, and that they had both become drug addicts while he, the husband, was away on a journey. Due to circumstances that are never revealed, the wife dies in a fire, together with another man, who strangely enough is not the painter with whom she had the affair, and nor is he of course her husband. In many ways *The White Cat* can be seen as the usual Ekman story but inverted. In almost all of Ekman's films there is a constant wish to escape the boredom of the mundane bourgeois life; to go abroad or become an artist or actor. That is also the case in *The White Cat*. However, this leads here to death and despair. In a confrontation between the husband, before he developed amnesia, and the painter, beautifully played by Sture Lagerwall, the painter says that he only wanted to be free, to be able to live life to its fullest potential, to be as creative as possible, and that he does not regret a thing. He then asks the husband if his life, the safe and secure one, was really worth living. The husband struggles to respond.

The film can be seen as taking place in the hidden corners, in the subcon-scious, of Ekman's characteristic dreamer. It is a subconscious filled with violence, sexual repression and neurosis, with the white cat a recurring symbol of a torn psyche. In one striking shot a white cat is seen crucified and in another scene a white cat is shot dead. Or is it another cat? It might be the same, like some kind of mystical creature. It keeps coming back, prowling the alleys, basements and attics, and haunting the characters' dreams. This is Ekman making a film in the style and with the ideas of 'Generation 40', which he had so many times criticised. This fact did not escape him. At one moment, the painter says to the husband that the situation he is describing is 'even worse than Generation 40…'. It could be argued that this does not really fit Ekman, and he struggles with the ending, trying to smooth over what has happened, in a sense introducing a ray of light into the prevailing darkness. During the title sequence the white cat is seen approaching the camera in an alley, but in the last shot the cat is seen running away from the characters and the audience along the same alley. Yet again, this is an example of Ekman's habit of beginning and ending the film in the same space, with an almost identical scene, but with a slight variation.

The critics were on the whole sceptical and felt that Ekman had failed to make a strong and coherent film, several critics suggesting that Ekman had tried to make a 'Bergman film' but since his heart was not really in it, and since he did not have the necessary depth, the end result suffered. There is a sense in which the critics were to some extent allowing their prejudice against Ekman to shape their responses, and Robin Hood felt the need to come to Ekman's defence. He wrote in a column that it was wrong to say that Ekman was a lightweight maker of comedies who now had tried and failed to make a serious film: 'He has within him more than just the spirited amiableness; he has also experienced life's unpleasant and dark sides. This foundation is what he wants to set free through his films. Has he not been at his most serious, most truthful as an artist exactly in those tough scenes in *The Banquet, Girl with Hyacinths, The White Cat*?' (Hood 1951, trans.).

What Robin Hood suggests here is that there has been a misreading, a misperception that Ekman is primarily a maker of comedies. The irony, however, is that even if Hood in this instance tried to set the record straight, the year before, in 1950, Hood had himself said that: 'Ekman began with light, shallow, graceful comedies, well made, and then changed his mind and became serious and realistic' (Hood 1950, trans.). But as has been made clear here, Ekman had always had this serious side, evidenced as early as his second film. Where this idea that Ekman was primarily a maker of comedies stems from is something of a conundrum; and it is still prevalent today. It might be due to Ekman's public appearances. Ekman was sometimes seen as a playboy, driving around in a yellow sports car and often seen with beautiful women, and maybe when critics thought about him as a film-maker they had this image in their heads. This image might then have skewed their memories of his films towards the funny and cheerful, much like a playboy. When he was asked in an interview if he considered himself a playboy the answer was that he certainly did not: 'No, I'm everything but a playboy. Work has taken up all my time. I wanted to work. Surely no playboy wants to do that?' (Frankl 1967, trans.).

Having said that, the other film in which Ekman was involved in 1950 was a comedy, *The Kiss on the Cruise*. It is tempting to view it as a distraction for Ekman, to do something light-hearted after the previous films. Although directed by Mattsson, it was based on an original idea by Ekman, who also wrote the script which the film follows closely. It was also marketed as 'the new film by Hasse Ekman'. It deserves to be discussed in connection with both Ekman and Mattsson but now the focus will be the Ekman connection. In the previous chapter the rivalry and competition between Ekman and Bergman was discussed and this competition was ongoing. There was a change, however, from *The Girl from the Third Row* to Ekman's approach in *The Kiss on the Cruise*, and in a few other films. These films were rather parodies of Bergman and Generation 40, unlike *The Girl from the Third Row*, which was more an intellectual engagement with Bergman. But *The Kiss on the Cruise* is not only a parody. It is also yet another example of Ekman's self-reflexive scripts.

The Kiss on the Cruise begins in Morocco (it is actually shot on location), where a group of children gathers around an elderly man who starts to tell them a story in Arabic about a filmmaker, faraway in the 'frozen North', who was married to an actress. The scene then shifts to a dingy apartment, where a man enters and starts to harass the older woman who lives there. He asks for a woman who is not there, whereupon he discovers a newborn baby in a crib. He immediately decides to murder the baby by drowning it. When the older woman objects he solemnly says 'We need to have the courage to be merciful!'; the woman raises her eyes and asks 'Is there no God?' and the man replies 'No, Clara-Bella...'. He then stops in mid-sentence and says: 'Oh, for crying out loud, I can't say these pathetic lines'. In this instance the audience realises that this is a film set, and that the scene was to be in a film. Then the director is shown wearing a beret, screaming and gesticulating. Few in the audience would at this point have failed to understand who this was supposed to be. It was a satiric portrait of Ingmar Bergman. If *The Kiss on the Cruise* is remembered at all today, it is for this parody of Bergman. To add an edge to this portrait, the director is played by Gunnar Björnstrand, who was one of Bergman's favourite actors (they made almost twenty films together). The sequence of the film-within-the-film has an additional level of meaning as well. It looks like the set of a film by F.W. Murnau, with crooked lines, low ceilings and forced perspectives. Murnau was undoubtedly one of the most influential of filmmakers of all time, and Bergman was one of many in whose work this influence can be seen. So when Ekman and Mattsson make the scene Murnau-esque, while keeping the dialogue Bergman-esque, they are making fun of Bergman in two ways: Bergman as an imitator of Murnau and Bergman as a writer of pretentious and pathetic dialogue.

After this sequence, and the ensuing argument between the actors and the director, there follows a lengthy sequence at the film set. The camera follows the director as he deals with set designers, actors, producers, the cameraman and others, who all seem to conspire against him, the great artist, and his vision. At one point he screams 'This is an artistic film! I don't want anything to be natural!', in another moment he sighs and says 'If only I had not turned down Hollywood, think of the resources and equipment they've got[!]', and finally he is off to give a lecture on 'the rebirth of cinema'.

The producer eventually persuades him to let his artistic ambitions rest for a while, and try and make a commercial comedy in exotic locations. This will be what the bulk of the film is about. It should at this point be clear that the similarities between this film and the previously discussed *Love and Downhill Racing* are considerable. They are both about struggling artists giving in to the demands from the studio to be commercial, and are slapstick comedies about mistaken identities and mad adventures taking place in exotic settings. These two films are of the type that the filmmakers in the films did not want to make, a case of Ekman trying to make fun of the cake while eating it. It comes to a point when it becomes almost impossible to separate fiction from fact, and it is perhaps not necessary to do so either.

The idea that the film is a parody of Ingmar Bergman should be nuanced. While it is true that in the beginning, the filmmaker character clearly represents Bergman making a 'Bergman film', there are also traces of Ekman in him (not least since Ekman had been compared to Bergman), and in a sense there is even something prophetic about the story, for later in the 1950s and early 1960s Ekman would himself be making the kind of international comedy in exotic locations he ridicules here.

The Kiss on the Cruise was directed by Arne Mattsson, but the credits begin with the words 'a film by Hasse Ekman', and as far as can be established by archival material both the idea and the script were Ekman's. The critics also mentioned only Ekman's name in their reviews, despite the fact that Mattsson was well established by this time (though his final breakthrough, commercially and artistically, would come the following year with *One Summer of Happiness*). In reviews of Mattsson's previous films, the critics held him responsible for whatever was good or bad in the respective films, but not this time. As mentioned with regard to *Love and Downhill Racing*, when Ekman was involved he would be the one singled out by the critics. In this case, the critics were not particularly pleased. They felt that *The Kiss on the Cruise* was awkward, not funny enough and condescending towards the south of Europe and North Africa. One critic wrote that: 'a certain smug tourist mentality towards the inhabitants of the various locations, who only get to act as buffoons, is spread unnecessarily wide' (Zack 1950, trans.) and it is true that the locals in both southern Europe and in North Africa are primarily seen as comic relief. But then again, few people in the film are seen as anything else. The Swedes are portrayed as being equally silly.

In Ekman's oeuvre, as well as in Mattsson's, *The Kiss on the Cruise* is a lesser film. But from an auteurist perspective it is very interesting. This is partly because it shows the strength of Ekman's presence even in a film directed by somebody else, and the consistency of his ideas (for example, the film is full of hidden and mistaken identities), and partly because it is another example of how the rivalry between Ekman and Bergman took place on screen as well as off it. Ekman's next film, *House of Madness* (*Dårskapens hus*, 1951), would also exemplify this.

As mentioned previously, a conflict between the film industry and the government led to strikes and an almost complete shutdown of filmmaking, which was called *filmstoppet*. During this period Ekman made a film which generated an angry debate in the media. Ekman took scenes and sequences from his earlier films and re-edited them so that together they made a new film, which he called *House of Madness*. The film is interesting for three reasons: first, because once again, it comments on the rivalry between Ekman and Bergman; second, because it shows off Ekman's skills as an editor; and third, because it gives an idea of how Ekman considered himself as a filmmaker.

The film begins in the year 2248, with a sequence in colour, when a society called 'Förening för Fornfilm Forskning' (The Society for Ancient Film Research) is explaining to the audience that they have found the remains of a film made three hundred years earlier, and directed by 'the master', Hasse Ekman. This film is said to be typical of the films the 'master' made in those days, a time of 'frenzy, crisis, thirst, lust and prison', and it is said that the film has the ability to 'move and to touch, to amuse and to disturb'. There then follows the black and white collection of scenes from previous films by Ekman, edited together so that they make a new film, with a new (and ridiculous) plot.

The words mentioned in the quote above, 'frenzy', 'crisis', 'thirst' and 'prison', are all titles of Bergman films, which is in itself interesting as yet another example of Ekman making fun of Bergman. What is more interesting is the way Ekman sees himself. If the film scholar from 2248 is to be seen as something of a spokesperson for Ekman himself then his speech is an insightful and relevant definition of Ekman's own work and style. He is defined as a filmmaker who handles serious subjects with a light touch; that is a very good description of the real Ekman, and his films do have the ability to move, amuse and disturb.

Even though a few critics enjoyed it, and were impressed by the editing, most disliked it and felt that it was an affront both to the actors, whose performances were taken out of context, and to Ekman's previous career. The one critic who liked it was Robin Hood. Most upset was Nils Beyer, who attacked the film, arguing that it was 'the most distasteful film that has ever been made in this country' (Beyer 1951, trans.) and that Ekman should withdraw it and make an official apology, primarily because of the way he had made a mockery of the actors and their performances. Ekman was defended by Harry Schein, in *BLM*. Schein argued that, although the film failed, the material Ekman used was 'both juridically and spiritually his' and he should be allowed to use it as he saw fit. Schein also felt that it could only do the actors a bit of good that somebody had some fun with them, and that the star cult in Sweden, even among critics, was unhealthy (Schein 1951, trans.). Schein's argument that Ekman had the juridical, moral and spiritual rights to the films is interesting in the context of authorship. Since Ekman often wrote, directed and produced his films, he had an unusually obvious claim to rights, and it could potentially be said that when the actors signed the contract to act in them, they gave up their rights. In any event it is difficult to see today what all the excitement was about, but it would have been interesting to hear the viewpoints of the actors. Bergman, when talking about the film in the 1990s, said that the problem with the film was that Ekman was being disrespectful towards his own films, and that there was an element of 'cynicism in that which was Ekman's only real failure', and for this reason he could not forgive Ekman for making it (Furhammar &

Åhlund 1993: 8, trans.). It is possible that Bergman's observations are accurate since, as has been shown previously, Ekman was filled with doubts about himself and his capabilities, and seems to have had low self-esteem; making fun of himself and his work may have been a sort of defence mechanism. Yet he continued to work, even though *House of Madness* met with perhaps the most hostile reception yet. Ekman has said that after having read the reviews he lost his self-respect (Ekman 1955: 211), but he was still not ready to give up making films.

The next project, *The Fire-Bird*, was something of a detour. It is a ballet film that was one of Lorens Marmstedt's European co-productions, and Ekman's first film in colour. It is clear that the global success of Powell and Pressburger's *The Red Shoes* (1948) had an influence on the film, as it had on so many other films of the time. It is not only the ballet setting which makes the films related but also the expressive use of colour, not least red. According to Furhammar, it was also the first Swedish feature film in which colour was used deliberately in an artistic way (Furhammar & Åhlund 1993: 13). It is a film set partly in Sweden and partly in Italy, with an international cast, and plays with the notion of national character-istics by using stereotypes and then transferring them. One example finds the traditional Swedish pastoral hymn 'Ack Värmeland du sköna' used first in a con-ventional, clichéd way in Sweden, and then later it is sung by an Italian in Italy, in broken Swedish.

The story is about the Italian opera singer Mario Vanni and the Swedish prima ballerina Linda Corina, their brief love affair, and the problems of combining life as an artist, at the height of success, with family life. As is so often the case in Ekman's films, the two worlds cannot mix: it is either art or family. It is also a somewhat traditional backstage story about the highly competitive world of ballet, with Linda Corina having to do battle with the up-and-coming ballerina Alice Lund, played by Eva Henning. Mario Vanni is played by the Italian opera singer Tito Gobbi, in one of only three films he made, the other two being Italian opera films. Linda Corina is played by Ellen Rasch, who was a professional ballet dancer and married to Marmstedt at the time. The ballet numbers were choreo-graphed by Maurice Béjart, one of Europe's leading choreographers. He was working in Stockholm at the time, although his great international fame was to come later in the 1950s.

The story is not unusual for an Ekman film, but that is not what makes the film interesting today. The interest stems rather from the ballet numbers and the artful use of colour. Ekman was again working with the cinematographer Göran

Strindberg, as well as Hilding Bladh, and the film is shot not in the commonly used Technicolor, but in Gevacolor. It was something of an experiment, and the Swedish technicians and laboratories were not equipped to handle it. Instead, the ballet sequences had to be developed in Paris, whereas part of the post-production was done at Denham Laboratories in Britain. The primary colour is red, which is the colour of the costume that the Fire-Bird, the main character in the ballet, is wearing. In fact, red is everywhere: a striking, bold and vibrant red that sometimes gives the film the impression of having been shot in 3D. Flowers, of which there are plenty, seem to be bursting out of the screen.

When Ekman was in Paris doing the post-production for *The Fire-Bird*, his wife, Eva Henning, left him. This was a great shock to him (Ekman 1955: 215–216) and it would affect his work. He dealt with the divorce in his plays and films, as will be discussed later; not, however, in the film which followed the international experiment of *The Fire-Bird*. His next film, *We Three Debutantes*, has already been mentioned, as the last part of the *folkhem* trilogy, and it is somewhat rare as Ekman himself was not credited with scriptwriting. According to the credits, Herbert Grevenius and Olof Molander wrote the script, but it seems reasonable to assume that Ekman had a hand in it as well. Grevenius had written the play it is based on, first performed on radio in 1941 but not on stage until 1948. It is a sweet and affectionate film, loosely structured and without any particular plot. It can be seen as a snapshot of life among the young in Stockholm during springtime in the early 1950s. The tone is set in the opening sequence, several minutes of images of Stockholm in the early morning sun, while Ekman introduces the film and the city with a voice-over. After this long, poetic sequence the audience is introduced to the three debutants, two young men and a young woman, who meet at a publishing house after it has been decided that their poems will be published together. One man is working class, the woman is middle class and the other man is upper class, and the hostilities between the two men are always simmering beneath the surface. However, the publisher is excited about the clash: 'The errand boy, hmm, bicycle messenger and the boss's son, what a publicity campaign, so *folkhemmet*!' Even though some of Ekman's earlier films dealt with the idea of *folkhemmet*, this is the one time it is explicitly mentioned.

The film touches on various aspects of class difference and without going into any particular depth it still creates a picture of ordinary life. The film shows that even after roughly thirty years of Social Democratic governments, class and gender are still unequal and co-existence is difficult. The three debutants have as their motto 'Together we stand, divided we fall', but sexual jealousies and class resentment mean that they fight more than they have fun, and in the end they go their separate ways, the working-class boy signing on with a ship bound for Ireland, because he cannot stand the suffocating life on land. On the one hand, it is a surprisingly pessimistic look at society, but on the other hand it remains consonant with Ekman's themes: the importance of freedom, the suffocating, judgemental nature of bourgeois society, and inequality between men and women. In this film, possibly because the original idea came from Grevenius and not Ekman, it discusses specifically Swedish topics; there is an unusually clear 'Swedish-ness' to it.

We Three Debutantes is also important because it inaugurates Ekman's permanent switch from Terra, where he had made most of his films thus far, to SF. The largest production company in Sweden, SF was more conservative and commercially inclined than Terra. *We Three Debutantes* is also the first film Ekman made together with the cinematographer Gunnar Fischer, who already had a successful working relationship with Ingmar Bergman and was one of Sweden's greatest cinematographers – comparable to Göran Strindberg. The films Fischer and Ekman made together are among Ekman's most stylish, although they are reminiscent of Ekman's work with Strindberg. Incidentally, Ekman and Bergman were competing over who could shoot the longest single take, and according to Leif Furhammar, Ekman won with a take in *We Three Debutantes* (Furhammar & Åhlund 1993: 14). The sequence takes place at an office and is 4.35 minutes long, with the characters and the camera moving back and forth around the office, introducing characters and instigating plot points.

The three debutants are played by Maj-Britt Nilsson, Sven-Erik Gamble and Per Oscarsson, and they were praised by the critics, as was the film as a whole. For some this was a comeback for Ekman, although the critic at the *Dagens Nyheter,* himself in the publishing business, disapproved of the portraits of the publishers. It must have been obvious to everybody in the business that the publishing house in the film was Bonniers, who also owned *Dagens Nyheter.* The two male poets in the film were inspired by real poets, particularly Harry Martinsson. At one point the three poets steal a rowing boat, an incident that was inspired by an actual occurrence. One of the poets involved in the actual theft was the aforementioned Stig Dagerman, the writer and occasional film critic who was part of Generation 40. Again and again, Ekman's habit of drawing upon the world around him is apparent, and in his next film, *Gabrielle,* this would be agonisingly clear. But before *Gabrielle* he wrote a script with Stig Olin, an actor turned director, for the film *Journey to You* (*Resan till dej*, 1953). Although co-written and directed by Olin, the film's theme, the difficulty of combining an artistic career with a relationship and family life, is similar to that of many of Ekman's own films. Here, Alice Babs plays an up-and-coming singer, and her husband, played by Sven Lindberg, is left behind when her career takes off. The film uses a number of techniques that would later be associated with the French New Wave, such as freeze-frames, self-conscious voice-over and even jump cuts, and although primarily shot in black and white (the cinematography is by Göran Strindberg), it also has musical daydreams which are in colour. Besides being technically interesting, it lacks the depth and passion of Ekman's best films.

As was mentioned earlier, Ekman's wife, Eva Henning, left him whilst he was in Paris doing the post-production work for *The Fire-Bird*. This was for him a great loss and he dealt with it artistically in several ways. Besides writing about it in his autobiography (which came out 1955), he wrote a play and made a film based on the experience. The play was called *Fullmåne* (*Full Moon*), and in it the Ekman and Henning characters eventually make up and get back together. It was a hit at Intima Teatern (Forslund 1982: 201) but the play was not made into a film. When he did make a film about the break-up it was not a hopeful and positive story, but a bitter and pessimistic one. The film was called *Gabrielle* and Ekman wrote it with Walter Ljungquist: it was their last film together. It is set in Paris, where Ekman was when the marriage collapsed, and tells the story of Bertil Lindström, a diplomat played by Birger Malmsten, who fears that his wife, Gabrielle, is about to leave him. Gabrielle, played by Henning, is not with him in Paris, but is visiting a small island in the Stockholm archipelago. The husband suffers from a combination of anxiety attacks and rampant jealousy, and in his head he is picturing what Gabrielle might be doing on the island in three different scenarios. In all three she is seduced by the same man, Kjell Rodin, played by Ekman, but each scenario ends differently. In one she and the man get together, in another she resists and in the third she tries to kill him. At the same time, in the actual world, the husband is waiting for a letter from his wife which will explain everything. Frustratingly, not least for the audience, he never gets to read what is in the letter, and when she comes to Paris to see him, their marriage ends.

The similarities between fact and fiction are rather clear, with the man trapped in Paris while the wife in Sweden is contemplating leaving him, and what is interesting is the difference between the above-mentioned play, *Fullmåne*, and the film *Gabrielle*. The play, written first, is wishful thinking, whereas the film is closer to the truth, and filled with despair. Typically for Ekman, however, the blame falls almost entirely on the man, and part of the problem is his jealousy. Several married men in Ekman's films are jealous, and often petty, whereas the characters played by Eva Henning and other actresses are usually more calm and collected, and in the comedies they laugh at their husband's or suitor's behaviour. But there is a special kind of sadness that fills *Gabrielle*, in that the man and the woman both want to be together, but since he is incapable of controlling himself, and is acting against his better judgement, he forces them apart.

Some critics, among them the influential Harry Schein at *BLM* and Nils Beyer at *Morgon Tidningen* (who three years earlier had attacked Ekman for *House of Madness*), thought *Gabrielle* was a great film, and as good as *Girl with Hyacinths*. Several others, while being dazzled by the visual and narrative complexities (one likened the film to a set of 'Chinese boxes'), felt that the theme of passion was beyond Ekman – that he was too nice and 'too well-brought-up' (Björkman 1954) to make a film about such matters. Yet again it is clear that Ekman's public persona was held against him as a filmmaker, despite the fact that he had made plenty of films filled with passion, emotion and angst. One critic wrote that the film might have been good had it been directed by Bergman. It sometimes seems as if the critics had a fixation with Bergman, and that Ekman, more than anybody else, suffered from this.

The narrative structure of *Gabrielle* was, as the critics noticed, fractured and complex, as so often with Ekman during these years, this time drifting not only back and forth in time, but also between dream and reality. The next film he wrote and directed, *Private Entrance* (*Egen ingång*, 1956), would be equally complex, and just as bitter and sad. *Private Entrance* was Ekman's first film of 1956 and has been seen by some, including Leif Furhammar, as proof that Ekman was losing his ability to make serious films. Furhammar writes that *Private Entrance*: 'unquestionably looked like a desperate and shameless, or perhaps embarrassed, effort to repeat the exclusive narrative structure that had been so successful in *While the Door Was Locked* ten years earlier, for lack of alternatives. It might have been acceptable had the effort succeeded, but now it did not' (Furhammar & Åhlund 1993: 14, trans.). Still, the film, albeit flawed, is very interesting and worthy of a closer look. It is interesting to note that it was originally to have been made by Bergman. *Private Entrance* is based on a book by a Norwegian writer, Sigurd Hoels, and the rights were bought by SF with the idea of letting Bergman direct it. Instead, Bergman then decided to make *Smiles of a Summer Night*, so the idea of filming Hoels's novel was suggested to Ekman, who took it on and rewrote the story.

Like several previous Ekman films, it begins with a voice-over and a shot of a house, on a particular street, Kavallerigatan 77. The speaker informs us that on this day Marianne Stenman will die, and he starts to tell her story and that of the events that lead to her death. The film yet again has a complex flashback structure with many characters, and is set in a milieu that Ekman knew well. Marianne Stenman (played by Maj-Britt Nilsson) is a model who marries a hard-working doctor at a large hospital. As he is never home and she feels neglected, she starts to see another man, Sture Falk, a journalist played by Hasse Ekman. He comes to her home to interview the husband, but as he is away the journalist and the wife start to talk and discover a mutual interest in art and painting (the home is filled with art, almost like a gallery), and they go to an exhibition of French painters on their first date. Then the plot moves back and forth between important events in her life and the present day. But the film is not only about her; it is about all the people in that building. As Furhammar mentioned, it is reminiscent of Ekman's earlier film *While the Door Was Locked*: the buildings are even on the same street. *Private Entrance* takes place on Kavallerigatan 77; in the earlier film it was Kavallerigatan 7. (There is no Kavallerigatan (Cavalry Street) in Stockholm. But Ekman lived on Artillerigatan (Artillery Street) when he grew up, so maybe he simply wished to retain the military theme.)

The main themes of the film are women's trials and tribulations in a male-chauvinistic society, the pettiness of ordinary people and the suffocating effects of the institution of marriage. The title refers to female empowerment and emancipation, suggesting that in order to be free women need to have their own entrance to the apartment, to the marriage. In the film, Marianne tries to break free from her marriage but after a month on her own the hatred with which she is met by her husband and her neighbours causes her mental breakdown, with the words 'Human beings are much more horrible than I thought' and her eventual, accidental death. It is an angry and pessimistic film, but the fact that a young couple, a student and an actress, still wish to get married in the end can be read as a measure of hope. It can also be seen as the final irony, that despite all evidence to the contrary, humans still persist in thinking matrimony is something intrinsically good. At one point the two young lovers are discussing a neighbour, and he says 'She's in all likelihood a good, proper wife', to which she replies, 'Proper? I can't imagine anything more boring!' – so maybe there is some hope for them. They also have an argument about her work in the theatre. He accuses her of neglecting him, saying 'But the theatre isn't everything, is it?', to which she replies: 'Yes, to me it is'. As should be clear by now, both of these sentiments return again and again in Ekman's films: the idea that respectability and propriety equal boredom and stagnation, that there is nothing more important than the theatre, and the strain this thinking often causes relationships. But it is not only the theatre. Marianne and her husband are genuinely in love at the beginning but what makes them enemies is the fact that he is always working, as he is a doctor at a hospital, and she is left alone. This scenario is reminiscent of the story in Ekman's earlier film *To Each His Own*.

Perhaps the most interesting debate in the whole film follows Marianne and the journalist's trip to the art exhibition:

Sture: *Life is ugly, art is beautiful.*
Marianne: *So all art is based on a lie?*
Sture: *No, but a great artist has the ability to create beauty that exists only in his imagination.*
Marianne: *Ridiculous. Isn't nature beautiful?*
Sture: *Yes, until man comes and destroys it. Between you and me, man is a bloody nuisance.*
Marianne: *Between you and me, you are a quasi-philosopher.*
Sture: *Between you and me, I'm hungry.*

This can be read as yet another instance of Ekman taking on Generation 40. It can also be seen as an outlet for Ekman of an inner conflict, between a deeply held view that the world is rotten, and a view that it should not be taken too seriously. It is not clear-cut, because the journalist speaking those misanthropic lines also talks about an ideal, which lies beyond right and wrong, beyond civilisation, and this is a sentiment that can be seen defended in several of Ekman's films, for example in the character of the vagabond in *Wandering with the Moon*.

Visually, *Private Entrance* is one of the most striking and inventive of Ekman's films, in part perhaps because of the cinematographer, Gunnar Fischer. The fact that it is raining outdoors in the scenes taking place in the present is put to expressive use in all interior shots, especially when Marianne is lying on a bed in a feverish condition. On the wall above the bed, and on the bed itself, is the reflection of a window. On the window, rainwater trickles down, making it appear that she is drenched, with water gushing over her. In another striking shot, the right part of the image is a close-up of the journalist's face and the left part is black. Then a superimposition of Marianne's face appears on the dark side of the image, and she speaks one line of dialogue. Then a new superimposition of her appears, and she speaks another line. This continues for some time, and it becomes almost like a condensed retelling of their whole affair, or as if her life is flashing before his eyes.

Another scene finds Marianne telling her husband that she is leaving him. His reaction is a combination of anger and self-pity, and they stand at opposite sides of the room, in medium shots, arguing. Then he starts to become really agitated and begins to gesticulate, and the camera stays on him, not cutting back to her. After a while the camera starts to track backwards, away from him. He slowly turns to follow the movements of the camera, and it can be assumed that it is moving towards the door, a suspicion that is confirmed by the sound of a door opening and closing. In this long take the camera becomes her, and we become her as well. Without her saying anything, and without her even being seen, the audience can feel and share her pity and loathing towards her loud and abusive husband.

So, *Private Entrance* is an important film, and essential when discussing Ekman's body of work. The problem with the film is that Ekman has included some unnecessary and melodramatic touches that jar with the rest of the film. The clearest example is the voice-over that appears frequently to remind the audience that Marianne has only a short time left to live. If the speaker had only introduced the film, it would have been fine, but coming back, again and again, the voice-over becomes a nuisance; an error of judgement.

Notes

1. There have been several theatres called Intima Teatern on different locations in Stockholm. One was open 1907–1910 and closely associated with August Strindberg, but these theatres have nothing in common other than their name.
2. In 2000, a Swedish medical journal published an article about *Girl with Hyacinths* and its importance in making homosexuality acceptable (Karlsson 2000).
3. Edith Södergran (1892–1923) was a Swedish-Finnish modernist poet. The lines come from the poem 'Färgernas längtan' (The Longings of Colours) and in Swedish they read: 'En tigerska ska jag vara i hela min levnad, / en talerska är som den sladdrande bäcken som förråder sig själv, / ett ensamt träd ska jag vara på slätten'.

CHAPTER 6

The Final Years

The last scene of *Gabrielle* takes place at Bromma airport in Stockholm. The character played by Hasse Ekman walks up to the desk that sells newspapers and magazines and he says '*Esquire, Look* and *Time* please. I'm flying to Brazil tonight'. It is the quintessential ending of an Ekman film, a lonely man buying international journals and then leaving Sweden for South America. Here the ending has some additional symbolism. A popular perception of Ekman's career among film historians is that it declined in the 1950s, that *Gabrielle* was the end of Ekman as a serious and successful artist. In *En liten bok om Hasse* Furhammar argues that in the years after 1953 Ekman did not: 'come even close to the wit, depth and passion of before' (Furhammar & Åhlund 1993: 14, trans.). Forslund argues that: 'There is really no need to talk about what Hasse did in the next 10 years – with a few *exceptions*' (Forslund 1982: 204, his italics, trans.). Gösta Werner argues along similar lines (Werner 1978: 92, 190).

As was explained in the first chapter, in the mid-1950s there was a decline in Swedish cinema in general and Ekman's *Gabrielle* can be seen as the last film of the Swedish renaissance. There definitely was a shift in Swedish cinema, and as described above, some have argued that there was also a shift in Ekman's career. The shifts in Swedish cinema and in Ekman's career might be related but the situation is more complicated when it comes to Ekman. It is clearly the case that something changed in Ekman's later films, beginning in 1956, but for it to be argued that this constitutes a decline there must be a valid definition of what is meant by 'decline'. As far as box-office success is concerned, it was not until the 1960s that the public began to lose interest in Ekman's films, and that could just as well be attributed to the changing habits of the public than anything specifically related to the quality of Ekman's writing or direction, as there was a general and catastrophic decrease in ticket sales, as mentioned in chapter 3. From the perspective of an auteurist study, there was no noticeable decline either. The themes and motifs that Ekman had been dealing with since 1940 were still there, and the films were mostly as personal as they had ever been. Whether they were qualitatively different, if the writing, direction and acting were worse than they had been, is a subjective issue. The later films in many filmmakers' oeuvres are often dismissed, or taken as evidence of decline. Charges similar to those directed against Ekman have been directed against many others, all over the world. While it is of course sometimes the case that a filmmaker declines, that the films are no longer good or successful, it is often more a question of the films being different and perhaps being seen to no longer fit the auteurist thematic models that the critics have established for them.

One of the purposes of this book has been to correct the lack of critical and scholarly attention given to Ekman's work. Yet, even if there has been little written about him in general, that which has been written relates to his work from the 1940s and 1950. There have been some books and essays covering those years, albeit to a very limited extent. But of Ekman's films made during the years covered in this chapter, 1956 to 1965, only the first two films under discussion (Ekman's last two films of 1956) have been written about in any depth. Therefore, there will be very few references to other texts in this section.

In 1956, Ekman made three films; one of them, *Private Entrance*, was discussed in the previous chapter. The other two films Ekman released in 1956 are very different from anything Ekman had done before, and it is significant that they were both made after the release of Bergman's *Smiles of a Summer Night* – significant because, after having seen *Smiles of a Summer Night*, Ekman sent a telegram to Bergman which read: 'I have just seen *Smiles of a Summer Night*. Now I give up. Just so you know. It is that bloody good!' (Forslund 1982: 205, trans.). This is not to say that Ekman necessarily would have continued making complex and artistic films had it not been for Bergman's successes, but as has been mentioned previously, Ekman had suffered both comparisons and criticism, which he found more and more difficult to handle. He had also lost Eva Henning, his life partner as well as his artistic partner. But instead of leaving for foreign shores, as so many of his film characters did, he turned a corner and moved on. At least for a while.

The filmmaker Schamyl Bauman and Ekman occasionally worked together and Bauman's 1930s output influenced Ekman. In 1955 Bauman became ill and could no longer make films. In a sense Ekman then took over what had been Bauman's filmmaking niche since the mid-1940s – that is, comedies starring the actress Sickan Carlsson. She was one of Sweden's biggest stars at the time and the type she specialised in was the sturdy and self-sufficient woman, who, although not immune to romance, had a more professional approach to love and life. In a way Carlsson was like a Swedish version of Doris Day. She and Bauman made nine films together between 1945 and 1955. Bauman had had a few weak years during the war but it could be said that he was rejuvenated by working with Carlsson, and the films were commercially successful but left the critics somewhat torn. However, they all agreed that Sickan Carlsson was sensational, a brilliant actress and a brilliant comedienne. It could be argued that the Bauman/Carlsson films were almost a particular genre. And the year after Bauman and Carlsson's last film together Ekman made his first with her: *Seventh Heaven* (*Sjunde himlen*, 1956). But the fact that the Bauman/Carlsson films were considered an institution does not mean that Ekman did not make the films his own. And it could be argued that Sickan Carlsson was just what Ekman needed after his recent setbacks.

Seventh Heaven is a travelogue of a bus journey around Europe, made in colour, full of music and with no apparent intent other than to amuse. It was the first of five films Ekman and Carlsson would make together, out of the fourteen films Ekman made after *Private Entrance* and that telegram to Bergman. Unusually, Ekman this time worked with Gustaf Molander's cinematographer Åke Dahlqvist, but of the sombre and carefully sculpted images of Molander's films nothing can be seen here.

Seventh Heaven begins, like several earlier Ekman films, with Ekman's own voice-over. A series of images of Stockholm ends with a shot of a man, and the voice-over introduces him: 'He did not know that twelve hours later he would lose his wife'. Then the scene changes to a radio studio where Willy Lorentz (played by Ekman) is about to start his new radio show, called *Seventh Heaven*. The aim of the show is to spread joy, happiness and love into the lives of the women of Sweden, in particular perhaps housewives, and it works. The show is a great success all over Sweden, and Willy Lorentz becomes an instant celebrity. One woman, however, is not impressed – the medical doctor Lovisa Sundelius (played by Sickan Carlsson) – but after initial hostility between the two they fall in love.

Foreign travel was something of a novelty in Sweden in the post-war era, and *Seventh Heaven* taps into this. The second half of the film takes place during a bus trip through Europe, from Stockholm to Rome, and the film feels as though it was co-funded by a travel agency or bus company. To further emphasise the element of novelty, one of the passengers on the trip at one point expresses his excitement about being on this journey. With a combination of wonder and a sense of regret he says: 'I'm sixty-five years old and I've never been outside of Sweden's borders'. The film can be seen as an effort not only to show the audience something they have not seen before – it is shot on location, in Hamburg, Heidelberg, Venice and all the way to Rome – but also to let the audience feel that they too can have this if they want, that there are now ways for them to travel abroad and that they should take this opportunity.

Seventh Heaven is rather frivolous and filled with crowd-pleasing elements but this does not negate Ekman's personal touches. It is also noticeable that *Seventh Heaven* is yet another of Ekman's films that is set in a creative milieu; in this case, radio. But whereas the theatre had always been treated with love and respect, this medium, the radio, was mocked on several levels. This was to be a recurring motif in subsequent Ekman films: the parody of popular media, including the biggest star of radio and television, Lennart Hyland. One reason for the disrespectful treatment of television and radio could be that they were a grave threat to both cinema and the theatre, since they took away their audience. But it could also be that Ekman felt that they encouraged conformity and bourgeois family life, since television and radio are media that are consumed in the home, with the family, rather than with strangers in a public place. The possibility of doing something spontaneous and unpredictable is perhaps higher if you are abroad in the world, rather than sitting at home with your family. This would be associated with the fear of boredom and stagnation that links so many of Ekman's characters.

Willy Lorentz, the character played by Ekman in *Seventh Heaven*, is not that far removed from the public face of the real Ekman, in that Willy Lorentz is playing a famous, easy-going playboy. But when that character is off the air, he complains about the commercialism and stupidity of the radio content in which he must participate. At one point he cries: 'I'll be damned if I'll have anything to do with this, you're making a fool out of me across the whole of Sweden'. He eventually has a nervous breakdown, and decides to quit. After being criticised for his show by Lovisa Sundelius, however, he gets so angry that he decides to continue with the show, and also tries to seduce her. In this endeavour he eventually succeeds, after he has genuinely fallen for her. She is struggling, however, in that the pair stands for two opposing worldviews. He stands for pleasure and life-affirmation; she stands for order and control, and is engaged to be married to a stiff officer (played by Gunnar Björnstrand). As has been argued on several occasions in this book, this is a key motif for Ekman: the perennial battle between the orderly and stable on the one hand and the life-affirming and spontaneous on the other hand. It is telling that it is not until Lovisa has left Sweden for a bus trip to Rome that she realises what a mistake marriage to her officer fiancé would be.

Her new-found sense of freedom, both in Bavaria and in Italy, is one important factor in her deciding to break off the engagement and run off with Willy Lorentz instead. In a sense her fiancé comes to represent Sweden, petty and correct, and Willy Lorentz the outside world, glamorous and exotic. This is of course a one-dimensional view of both Sweden and Continental Europe, but it is important to remember that it is not so much Italy in itself that is exciting and exotic, but the fact that there is a world outside Sweden, a world which might be less meticulously designed and safe, and is therefore more alive. In this film, as in so many earlier Ekman films, the argument is that bourgeois ideals are overvalued, including respectability and responsibility.

So here, the personal interests of Ekman, the studio's need for a box-office success and the travel agencies' wish to promote charter trips for the working and middle classes coalesced. The film became both a sign of the times and yet another expression of Ekman's deeply held beliefs. And it was a huge hit (Forslund 1982: 206). Some critics saw it as a return for Ekman from the gloom of *Private Entrance* to the cheerful comedy of *Seventh Heaven*. However, one critic pointedly wrote: 'Hasse may be very angry with the comparison, but Ingmar would have placed the same sequences on a completely different artistic level – occasionally during the course of the film this acknowledgement feels like a lamentation' (Björkman 1956, trans.). It is certain that Bergman would have made the film differently, but there is no reason to think it would have been better. Bergman was not incapable of a bad film. It is also somewhat strange that the critics felt that it was a return to form for Ekman after his previous, tragic film. He had, after all, not made a comedy since *One Swallow Does Not Make a Summer* in 1947, so if this was a return to form for Ekman it would imply that all the films made in between, such as *The Banquet*, *The Girl from the Third Row*, *Girl with Hyacinths* and *Gabrielle*, were just a waste of time.

Whereas *Seventh Heaven* is symptomatic of Ekman's films from then on – glossy releases with Sickan Carlsson – the other comedy of 1956, *Ratataa or the Staffan Stolle Story*, is rather different and could be seen more as belonging to Ekman's theatre work than his film oeuvre. That is not to say it is not a cinematic film, but he made it together with the revue ensemble Knäppup. Knäppup consisted of Povel Ramel, Martin Ljung, Gunwer Bergkvist, Brita Borg and other comedians and singers, and this group was both popular and influential in Swedish music and comedy and on stage. Ekman would work with them on several occasions. *Ratataa* is a strange hybrid of musical, biopic, parody and comedy, and it demonstrates his abilities as a storyteller and deft handler of the camera. He was again working with Åke Dahlqvist, and this time the cinematography is more artistic than in *Seventh Heaven*. It is also yet again partly a parody of Bergman, in this case of *Smiles of a Summer Night*. The film is set at the same time and in the same milieu as Bergman's film, with both specific scenes and lines of dialogue clearly, and cleverly, taken from Bergman and then twisted around. This was, however, the last time such a Bergman parody would appear in any film by Ekman.

The story tells of the nobleman Staffan Lefverhielm (played by Ramel), who after a failed duel with his arch-enemy Klåd Tränger (played by Ekman) is sent off to the tropics, together with his friend Vicke Wickberg. After having languished in a little restaurant, in a location reminiscent of the setting of the French film *The Wages of Fear* (*Le salaire de la peur*, Henri-Georges Clouzot, 1953), they move back to Stockholm and start careers as entertainers, singers and composers. As with *The Fire-Bird*, the story is of no particular interest here, despite again being about artists, but it is the inventiveness and madcap humour that should be noted. Furhammar has argued that the film is 'a small masterpiece' and 'flawless' (Furhammar & Åhlund 1993: 32–34, trans.); many critics at the time found it a funny, even hilarious film, especially the musical numbers, and they tried to name all the different films that were being parodied along the way. In chapter 4 of this book a critical attack on Ekman by some critics was discussed. Ekman was accused of being a bartender, stealing from other films, instead of making something original. Even though the criticism is unfair, and Ekman's response was pertinent, it is as if, in making *Ratataa*, Ekman had taken to heart the criticism that he had received but decided to turn it into a virtue, taking it as a challenge instead. So in a way, Ekman got the upper hand.

The next year, 1957, when Bergman made *Wild Strawberries* (*Smultronstället*) and *The Seventh Seal* (*Det sjunde inseglet*) – two films that circulated in the wider world and quickly became recognised as classics of world cinema – Ekman made *Country House Wanted* (*Sommarnöje sökes*; the Swedish title has a double meaning in that *sommarnöje* can mean either a country house or a summer fling), a low-key comedy which was not released abroad. As far as the domestic audience was concerned, Ekman triumphed, with *Country House Wanted* becoming his most commercially successful film. It tells the story of a family of three: husband, wife and daughter. The wife and daughter are out in the archipelago while the father is in town working, and there he gets romantically involved with another woman. At the same time both wife and daughter are interested in a reclusive man, a painter, who lives on the island where they are renting a house. They keep their passions under control, however. In town the mistress moves in with the husband and they play a game, pretending they are married. This is perhaps the one Ekman-esque touch that really stands out in the film, with people hiding behind a mask, playing parts instead of facing reality. Eventually, the real wife finds out about the affair but instead of being angry, she finds it somewhat sweet. When she learns that her husband has broken up with the mistress over the telephone, she feels for her and invites her out to the island to celebrate the husband's birthday. There the original couple get back together, while the ex-mistress is wooed by the painter.

Whilst not particularly striking, *Country House Wanted* is amiable enough and displays Ekman's relaxed attitude to society's conventions. Nobody is being judged here. However, if the wife had also had an affair that was shown in the same forgiving light, the film would have been more daring. It could be dismissed as a man's fantasy but what saves it is that the extramarital affair is shown as being real and affectionate, and perhaps even necessary to save a marriage that had grown stale. The play-acting between the husband and mistress is actually touching. It is worth pointing out that the three lead actors were part of Bergman's stock company. The husband and wife were played by Gunnar Björnstrand and Eva Dahlbeck, and the daughter was played by Bibi Andersson.

Country House Wanted was shot by Martin Bodin, and he would be the cinematographer for all of Ekman's remaining films. Like *Seventh Heaven*, this was shot in Eastman Color, as would be the case with all Ekman's remaining colour films. Also like his previous film, it is executed in subdued colours, far from the exuberance of *The Fire-Bird*.

The next film Ekman made, *The Halo is Slipping* (*Med glorian på sned*, 1957), was his second with Sickan Carlsson. As usual, she plays an efficient, independent and self-sufficient professional woman, and this time she is in publishing. She is married but takes no pleasure in her marriage. Instead she writes a book under a pseudonym and sends it to the publishing company she is working for. The book is about her life, and reveals that she loves her boss, the chief editor at the publishing company, played by Ekman. The title of the book is *The Powerlessness of Honour*, and it becomes an instant bestseller, generating much publicity. Eventually she breaks up with her husband and marries her boss.

Again, the film rehearses the dichotomy of creativity versus domestic boredom, with a strong woman at its centre, but especially noteworthy here are some dream sequences. When making *Ratataa*, Ekman had begun collaborating with the comedian, artist and sometime filmmaker Yngve Gamlin, and Gamlin would make elaborate set designs for a number of films by Ekman from then on, specialising in dream and dance sequences, moments that would visualise the subconscious of the characters and imply symbolic meanings. Here are links between the new ideas in design and art that were popular in Sweden at the time.

Up to that point, there was no sign of any decline in Ekman's work. These last three films might have been different from most of the films he had made before 1956, but the question of decline compared with his earlier comedies was not an issue for either the critics or the spectators. The films were witty and well-acted and full of Ekman's recurring themes. They were as personal as ever. The next film, though, was in some ways seen as a disappointment.

Bergman and Ekman were then colleagues at Sweden largest studio, SF, and the rivalry was perhaps contained. From this point on they would be more supportive of one another, and Ekman would not make any more films that were parodies of Bergman, or that criticised him. After Ekman had admitted defeat in the telegram to Bergman, he perhaps felt less stressed and less competitive and could take pleasure in Bergman's successes instead. However, the fact that both Bergman and Ekman were working for SF has prompted Leif Furhammar to observe that 'it must have felt a bit strange [for Ekman] to be the one at SF who with his professional routine more than anyone else created the financial support for the artistic freedom of his former rival, Bergman' (Furhammar & Åhlund 1993: 29, trans.). There is no denying the irony in this. In his 1958 film, Ekman would yet again touch upon their relationship but this time neither in a philosophical way, as in *The Girl from the Third Row*, nor as parody, as in the films discussed in the previous chapter. It would be in a more resigned way, in a way acknowledging the defeat, but this does not make it any less interesting. The film was called *The Jazz Boy*.

The Jazz Boy got its name from a very popular song of the 1920s called 'Jazzgossen', a number which features in the film. Ekman's film is an ambitious undertaking, a combination of musical and historical biopic of a fictional character, made with a large budget. It seeks to capture the evolution of Swedish show business from the early 1920s until the Second World War. That it is a film close to Ekman's heart might be deduced from the fact that the main character is called Teddy Anker, that name making its fourth appearance in Ekman's films. There are also many people playing themselves: figures who are skilfully integrated into the story. Many well-known singers and writers appear, for example Karl Gerhard, who was introduced in chapter 2.

The Jazz Boy was the first time Ekman made a film that was not shot in Academy ratio (1.37:1). Instead it was a widescreen production, with an aspect ratio of 1.66:1. It might have been expected that a film such as *Seventh Heaven* would have benefited from being in widescreen, with its ambitions to show off the sights of Europe, but for some reason it was shot in Academy ratio. *The Jazz Boy* was again an Eastman Color production, but the cinematography by Bodin is not inspiring, despite the film having musical numbers. Yet from a historical perspective, *The Jazz Boy* is more interesting, especially for the purposes of this study. The film covers the period during which Ekman grew up, one which was an important era in Swedish show business. In addition, the film is rich in typical Ekman themes and touches. During the title sequence, a man is seen tap dancing towards the camera on what looks like a large, white stage. After this title sequence, there is a cut to a plate with the numerals 1922, and when the camera zooms out it is revealed that it is the number plate of a Stockholm car (in those days the number plates were organised after the district they came from, and all Stockholm cars had number plates beginning with an A). The car's owner is Teddy Anker (who is played by Ekman) and he is on his way to watch a show. Driving there, he almost runs over a young woman (played by Maj-Britt Nilsson). Her name is Karin Ingel and as an apology he drives her to the place where she is going, a lecture about communism. Karin is dating Erik Jonsson, a poet and communist, and she asks Anker if he is interested in politics, to which he replies: 'As the good little jazz guy I am I prefer Karl Gerhard to Karl Marx'. Later that night, while Karin is at home listening to her boyfriend's poems, Anker buys a small nightclub. Unbeknownst to him, Karin starts to work as a dancer at the nightclub, and eventually she leaves her boyfriend for Anker, and they get married.

As Anker's show-business empire grows, so does his recklessness. Business is good so he is making a lot of money, and he is willing to take whatever chances he can. He is working all the time, and neglecting his wife. Simultaneously he also forces Karin to become his star, making the first Swedish talking picture with her in the lead, and trying to make her a theatre star as well. But it fails, partly because she is not good enough, and at the same time their marriage deteriorates. Besides investing in his own business, Anker has also invested a lot in Kreuger stocks. Ivar Kreuger, who was discussed in chapter 2, was a Swedish businessman and investor, and since he was interested in films, he invested heavily in the Swedish film industry as well as in more traditional industries. At one point in the film, when two characters are discussing Kreuger, it is said that he was 'pumping gold into welfare-Sweden'. Then comes the so-called Kreuger crash, leading to his suicide in Paris in 1932. In a telling scene in the film, at a performance of one of Anker's shows a member of the audience is given a piece of paper. He immediately gets up and forces his way out of the row, while people start to whisper to each other, and as soon as anybody is told what was written on the paper they too get up and leave. Eventually, the camera moves close to the paper lying on the floor and the message reads 'Kreuger is dead'. This is the beginning of the end for Anker and his professional career. After having sold everything, and finding himself alone, he leaves for Africa.

Then comes the Second World War and Anker returns home, becoming a soldier. In the end he meets Karin again, briefly. After they have said goodbye he turns his back towards the camera and walks further and further away, in a white space. It is a shot reminiscent of the opening shot of the film, as is so often the case in Ekman's films, only this time the subject is not tap dancing in the middle of a white stage, but walking in deep white snow, leaving a trail of lonely footprints behind.

As this résumé of the plot should have made clear, it is in many ways a typical Ekman story, set in the world of performers and the stage. Some of the characters in the film are playing themselves, and many are based on real people. It also has that conflict of stability and security versus impulsiveness and excitement which runs through the whole of Ekman's oeuvre. This time the impulsiveness and excitement lead to a bitter end. It could be argued, however, that it might not matter all that much that the end was brutal. As was articulated in many earlier Ekman films, it is better to have really lived for a while than to have spent a whole life secure and embalmed.

Another recurring feature in Ekman's films is art: artists, painters and paintings, which appear so frequently as to become a theme in their own right. There is a painting in *The Jazz Boy* that has symbolic value. The first time Karin comes to Anker's apartment she notices a large painting by the Swedish rural painter Anders Zorn. As they are looking at it a piece of music is faintly heard in the background, music which is from the same time as the painting was painted, and from the same region in Sweden, and Karin says that the woman in the painting was her grandmother. This painting appears later in the film, on a number of occasions, and in a way follows the couple through their life together. Paintings also feature prominently, to the extent that they almost become a part of the plot, in *We Three Debutantes*, *Private Entrance* and *Ratataa*. There are painters in prominent roles in *Happiness Approaches*, *One Swallow Does Not Make a Summer*, *The Girl from the Third Row*, *Girl with Hyacinths* and *The White Cat*, and in these films paintings also have special functions. The question then becomes whether these painters and paintings have a deeper meaning. At the end of *The Jazz Boy*, one of the things Anker has to do is to sell his large art collection. How many of those paintings were owned by Ekman himself is difficult to say, but the auction scene would recur in real life a few years later. In his private life, Ekman was an avid art collector, filling his home with paintings, primarily by modern Swedish artists. When he left Sweden and moved to Spain in 1964 he sold the collection for SEK705,700 (Forslund 1982: 227), which today (2016) would be around SEK7 million (or £600,000). It is possible that the paintings in the films were partly a way for Ekman to show off his own collection. Some of his characters seem to live in a gallery, such as Marianne Stenman in *Private Entrance*. But it is more than this. Ekman uses art to define characters, and to say something about them. Painters and paintings for Ekman are not just for decoration or for commerce: they are essential, both to his own art and to his views of the world, people and relationships. Paintings hang on the wall not just because they are beautiful but because they say something vital about the person in whose apartment they are hanging, such as the painting of the two women in Dagmar Brink's apartment or the painting *The Scarecrow*, also known as *Death and the Girl*, by Nils Dardel, which hangs on the wall at the home of the masochistic couple in *The Banquet*. When watching Ekman's films, paying attention to the artworks displayed, the frames within the frames, can be very rewarding.[1]

To return to *The Jazz Boy*, Erik Jonsson, the man Karin is originally dating but leaves for Anker, is partly inspired by Bergman – not that Bergman was a communist, but they share other traits. On one of their dates Erik reads her his poems, which are pessimistic and tragic. 'It is as if death was the most beautiful thing in life for you', she says, and he answers that he does not know why he has these thoughts, an allusion to Bergman's well-known focus on death in his own work. Erik and Anker are seen as rivals, and initially Anker wins Karin, but after she and Anker break up she goes back to Erik and they get married, with him having secured a job at the Royal Dramatic Theatre in Stockholm. This makes it even more tempting to see Erik Jonsson and Teddy Anker as related to Bergman and Ekman, and Karin as a symbol of their rivalry, not over the same woman, but over their status in Swedish cultural circles at the time, with Bergman now the committed artist and Ekman the lightweight entertainer. This conflict between art and commerce would appear again, in somewhat unusual circumstances, in Ekman's next film.

The Great Amateur (Den store amatören, 1958) is not set in Stockholm, but in a small (fictional) town called Fårtuna, and the view of the town is initially condescending. Most of the people who live there are presented as backward and silly, but the small town is also seen as threatening. When two men from Stockholm accidentally end up there, one of them says: 'It's not a town, it's like a panopticon. No wonder people are fleeing from the countryside'. The two men are Max Wallby, a theatre owner played by Ekman, and his assistant, Roffe, played by Sven-Eric Gamble, and while staying in town they come across an amateur theatre company. Wallby falls for the lead actress, Linda (Marianne Bengtsson), and tries to persuade her to come to Stockholm and play at one of his theatres. Her response is uncharacteristic for an Ekman character: 'I'm not sure I really want to act; I would rather dance. I love to dance'. But she cannot relinquish the dream of going to the city, and struggles with her sense of responsibility towards her home town and the lure of the city. The dichotomy between town and country is played out in the ballet numbers that are spread through the film, with the girl at one moment playing the role of the city, dancing gracefully, opposite a man playing the country, coming across as clumsy. In another ballet she is playing the part of a girl caught between the two sides. She does eventually move to the big city, and begins to work on the stage for Wallby (the productions are lavish, and he calls it 'neonrealism'). But what makes The Great Amateur so rare is that this time the small town eventually wins. Alfred, the head of the small-town theatre company, who is in love with Linda, follows her and tries to get her back. In the end she decides to stay with him, leaving the city behind.

As well as running the amateur theatre group, Alfred is the local police constable. In one scene he has taken Wallby in for questioning, and is interrogating him in his office. When Alfred finds out that Wallby also works in the theatre he says: 'But then we are like colleagues. What kind of theatre?' Wallby replies: 'Mostly musicals and shows'. Alfred looks disappointed and says: 'So, the easy option, just to make money'. Wallby answers: 'Yes, and to some extent entertain'. Alfred is becoming more judgemental, but Wallby answers, 'It's much easier to be an idealist in your position than in mine', and defends his line of business partly on the grounds that many people are depending upon him to bring in money. It is easy to read this as yet another instance of Ekman working out his real-life battles in his film scripts and defending himself against the critics (or possibly himself). The fact that this scene takes place in a police station gives it an almost paranoid quality, as if Wallby is being arrested for being commercial. Whether or not Ekman was consciously thinking about these matters when he wrote and shot the scene is not known, and it does not matter. The interpretation is still there to be drawn, and it shows how the view of Ekman as an internal auteur can give a broader perspective when analysing the films.

Martin Ljung, who played Alfred, the policeman and amateur actor, was a member of Knäppup, the comedy group that Ekman had worked with before on *Ratataa*. Yngve Gamlin, who designed the dream and dance sequences here as well as in *The Halo is Slipping*, was also a member of Knäppup. This was to be their last co-operation on a film set, even though Ekman and Knäppup would work together onstage, up to the 1970s. For his next film, Ekman returned to Sickan Carlsson.

Miss Chic (*Fröken Chic*, 1959) was a great success, financially as well as criti-cally; one critic even called it a comic masterpiece (E.L. 1959). This time Sickan Carlsson plays Isabella, a teacher who is also an expert on popular music and as such she is competing in the television quiz show *Kvitt eller dubbelt*. (*Kvitt eller dubbelt*, Double or Nothing, was a real quiz show which was broadcast on Swedish television for the first time in 1957, inspired by the American show *The $64,000 Question*.) Ekman himself plays an artists' agent who has no clients any more, but when he realises that Isabella will be a big hit, he tries to get her to sign up with his agency.

Miss Chic, besides being Ekman's first film shot in Aga-Scope, a Swedish ver-sion of CinemaScope, is primarily focused on making fun of television, and espe-cially the host of *Kvitt eller dubbelt*, Nils Erik Bæhrendtz. In the film he is played by Stig Järrel, and called Docent Urbàhn (the name is a play upon the Swedish surname Urban, as well as the word 'urban'). Overall, the tone of the film is Wodehousian and in that way it recalls some of Ekman's films from the early 1940s, as well as being one of his most Lubitsch-esque films. But it is also a satire on masculinity, offering a light-hearted kind of feminism where Ekman's charac-ter, Buster Carell, and other male characters too, are constantly upstaged and ridiculed by a series of strong and forceful women, including a female judo team which uses Buster Carell for practice. The film is also another of Ekman's evoca-tions of the world of showbiz and creativity. It is unevenly paced (unusually for

Ekman, it is slow and laboured), and the editing is not as sharp as it usually is, which is probably due to the new widescreen format Aga-Scope, which might have made filming more difficult in the beginning. But even so there is little evidence of decline. *Miss Chic* was after all called a comic masterpiece and it is still popular today. The next film, however, was a rare disaster, critically as well as financially.

In an effort to play it safe, Ekman now returned to the subject of television, returning also to the characters from *Seventh Heaven*. In *Great Scott!* (*Himmel och pannkaka*, 1959, the title literally means 'Heaven and Pancakes', which is an old-fashioned Swedish expression of surprise), Willy Lorentz, the radio star from *Seventh Heaven*, has become a television star and is being marketed as the rival to Lennart Hyland. Lorentz has the same producer (Stig Järrel) and writer (Sigge Fürst) as previously, and he is still married to Lovisa Sundelius (Carlsson). The film is worth mentioning only for the fact that this is the only film of Ekman's which actually takes place in Latin America, more specifically in Guatemala. The film was part-financed by the Swedish Banankompaniet (The Banana Company) and they paid for the trip across the Atlantic. It might be asked whether there was any reason to make it other than to get a free trip to South America. The film is full of what today is called product placement, but in a self-conscious way, to make fun of the practice. This is reminiscent of the way Ekman handled some film scripts before. When doing a ridiculous project he would write it as a self-conscious comment upon its own deficiencies, and parody the very film he was making, and *Great Scott!* could easily be compared with *Love and Downhill Racing* and *The Kiss on the Cruise*, two films that were discussed earlier.

Be that as it may, *Great Scott!* was not a hit. The year 1956 had been a spectacular year for Ekman, in terms of box-office receipts, with the release of three of his four most successful films: *Ratataa*, *Seventh Heaven* and *Country House Wanted*, the fourth most successful being *Little Märta Steps Forward* from 1945 (Forslund 1982: 215), but those days were over. This decrease in ticket sales was partly because television had taken its toll, but perhaps also because Ekman's films lacked the sex and provocation of Bergman's films or the excitement of Arne Mattsson's thrillers: those two filmmakers continued to be popular.

For his next film, Ekman brought back Eva Henning. The last time they had worked together was in 1954 when they had made *Gabrielle*, the film inspired by the breakdown of their own marriage. She had not made any films since then and she would not make any more with Ekman apart from this one, *Decimals of Love*

(*Kärlekens decimaler*, 1960). Ekman plays a golf coach, Charlie Gedelius, who is working abroad because he has fallen out with his family. When the film begins he is in Denmark and there he meets Lena Lind, played by Henning. He falls for her, but she is going up to Sweden to get married to his brother. He decides to go home too, to try and get back together with his family. Since the family is wealthy, instead of telling them the truth about himself, he more or less invents a persona that he then presents to them, saying that he is rich and successful. His family, on the other hand, whilst actually rich and successful, are not particularly happy. They are merely going through the motions. His brother wants a divorce so that he can marry Lena Lind, the same woman Charlie wants, but they are all living lives based on lies, and they are all unhappy together. Eventually, Charlie, after having made peace with them, cannot take that kind of life any more. He has been offered a job in Barcelona, and in the end he leaves his family again and flies to Spain. He makes a stop on the way to visit a friend in Denmark, and he tells the friend that he is moving to Spain with Lena.

Had *Decimals of Love* been Ekman's last film it would have been very fitting in terms of how it relates to his earlier films. It took at its subject several of his main concerns that were well established by then: the seeming inevitability of married, comfortable life leading to stalemate and boredom, and how common, and easy, it is to live a lie rather than an authentic life. Charlie says at one point: 'We all pretend to be better than we are, and if we did not we would probably not have the strength to carry on'. And in the end he gives up, and moves to Spain. As in *Happiness Approaches, Changing Trains, While the Door Was Locked, The Banquet, The Girl from the Third Row, Girl with Hyacinths* and *Private Entrance*, people's lives are compromised by society's conventions and the inhibitions they bring with them, unless they are among the brave few who battle against them. Those who will not battle, usually because they do not have the strength, instead take comfort in the lie. So it is in *Decimals of Love*. Here Charlie takes a lie with him. Even though the audience is meant to believe that Lena is going with him, and even though he tells his friend in Denmark that she is, in the last shot it is revealed that this, too, was a lie. She did not come with him, she did not want to be with him after all, and he is going south alone.

Despite the many strengths and interesting aspects of the film, the critics were not in the least impressed, and as this quote, from the critic Carl Björkman in *Dagens Nyheter*, suggests, the times had changed: 'Decimals of Love is one of the many Swedish films that are insufferable because they are in a sense untouchable. One of these films that make you scream for imagination and a willingness to try new things, for boldness and God knows what. A film that makes you want to scream for a Swedish New Wave' (Björkman 1960, trans.). The film that could arguably be said to be the first in such a new wave, *The Pram* (*Barnvagnen*, 1963) by Bo Widerberg and Jan Troell, was just around the corner. It is worth noticing, however, that when *The Pram* was released, it was criticised for trying too hard to be new and fresh. What can be said of *Decimals of Love* is that it is conventional in style, with none of the technical playfulness and inventiveness of other films of the time, or even of earlier films by Ekman. It neither has any provocative language or scenes nor is about youth or aiming for a young audience. But another aspect of the many global new waves was their personal touch and whatever other flaws *Decimals of Love* may have had, it was definitely personal. It even seems like an act of masochism to have brought back Eva Henning. But as with *Gabrielle*, Ekman did not try to make the world on film prettier than it was in reality. In the film, she does not want him, and does not go with him to Spain.

After the colour and Aga-Scope of *Great Scott!*, Ekman returned to Academy ratio for *Decimals of Love*, and for his next film, *On a Bench in a Park* (*På en bänk i en park*, 1960), he also gave up on colour, possibly because colour was too expensive at this time. The setting for *On a Bench in a Park* is the theatre, and with the combination of black and white, Academy ratio and theatre, in a way it was a return to the 1940s. The script moves back and forth between what is happening on the stage and what is happening in the real world and it has some of those intertextual aspects that make Ekman's films so interesting. The play that the theatre is mounting is a commercial project because it is in desperate need of money – as is the owner of the theatre, Stig Brender, played by Ekman. In the beginning, while they are rehearsing the new play, one of the old actors suddenly gets up and leaves because he has had enough, and he feels 'disgust towards selling out to the audience like this'. Brender manages to persuade him to stay.

Ekman too stayed on, for four years and three more films, and while they adhered to the same format and monochrome, they were very varied. Unusually, the next one, *The Heist*, was not written by Ekman but by Jan-Olof Rydqvist, his only credited script. At the time, 'the teenager' had emerged as an important demographic in Sweden, and teenagers were not interested in sitting at home in front of the television. They preferred the cinema, making them a new target audience. In a sense, teenagers went to the cinema to see films about teenagers

(Furhammar 1991: 250–252), and *The Heist* spoke to this audience. It is perhaps the only film among those Ekman made after 1956 that is somewhat in tune with the time in which it was made and this is obvious even from the first shot. It is a conventional panorama shot over Stockholm, but the music is different. The film has an energetic jazz score (the music is by Rune Öfwerman), which was a first for Ekman, but consonant with a growing trend in French, British and US films of the period. *The Heist* follows two criminals who escape from jail in the opening sequence, and then decide to pull one last job that will give them enough money to move abroad and live a life of luxury. It is a traditional storyline, but what gives it its edge is the impressive cinematography, combined with the score and the depth of the characters. The film has a certain existential angst, which links it to Ekman's earlier films of the 1940s and early 1950s. In the middle of the film, the only time when the two convicts are not running or fighting, they have settled down to rest in a safe apartment. They have also picked up a few girls. The younger of the two men, played by Gunnar Hellström, and one of the girls, played by Maude Adelson, are having an intimate moment, more emotional than sexual as they have both finally met someone who understands them. Both have a feeling of being trapped, a sense of imprisonment which follows them around wherever they go. Family and society imprison them, and the girl at one point describes her existence as: 'like a nightmare, and you want to wake up, only it's not possible to wake up'. At the end of the film, when the two men are cornered by the police in Copenhagen, the girl is asked by the police to tell them to surrender. There then is a shot of the girl, dressed in white, standing on a square in a pool of darkness, surrounded by policemen. It is a haunting image of loneliness, fragility and entrapment, and one of the most striking visual expressions of what so many of Ekman's characters, mostly women, feel so very often.

Despite the fact that Ekman was more in tune with the prevalent cinematic fashion when he made *The Heist* then he had been for a few years, he was still criticised in the reviews. The critics felt that it was now too long since he had made anything really important and worthwhile. They were critical not only of Ekman but of the climate in Swedish cinema, and one critic formulated these sentiments thus:

> Hasse Ekman of course knows his profession. But it is a very long time since he has had a particular agenda. Once upon a time he was very polished and bitter; there was a foundation in what he did, which was interesting and unsettling.

It is a pity that he has become tired and sidestepped his problems.
Understandable but lamentable. It is often said about Nehru that he is like a
very large tree that towers over everything and in that way suffocates all that
is growing in its vicinity. The same can apparently be said about Ingmar
Bergman. There remains no vegetation either beside or under [him]. And it is
needed. For the benefit of everybody. (Höken 1961, trans.)

The Heist did actually have strong connections with Ekman's earlier films, where
he was 'polished and bitter'. The alleged decline in Ekman's work can be said to be
more in the minds of the critics and scholars than in the actual films that were
made. He had been making films for twenty-two years by then, but he was still true
to his themes and his beliefs, he had continued to make personal films, and the
overall quality of the films is very strong. There had been occasional setbacks,
films that were not as good or as popular as the best, but they were temporary, and
always followed by something that was very good, and/or popular. So it could
actually be argued that rather than showing signs of decline he showed signs of
remarkable consistency and stamina. But he would make only two more films after
The Heist.

   My Love is Like a Rose (Min kära är en ros, 1963) was a drama, photographed by
Gunnar Fischer and based on a play by Bo Sköld, who also wrote the script. No
film by Ekman has received such bad reviews and today the film, because of rights
issues, is unavailable, even in the film archives. (It was viewed just once for this
study at a closed screening at the Swedish Film Institute.) The film seems like an
effort on Ekman's part to try something new. It is not like any of his other films:
rather, it is reminiscent of Michelangelo Antonioni's work, stylistically and thematically. It has a geometric precision in the images and is about middle-class
people feeling alienated and lost. One screening is not enough to analyse it further, but it is still worth noting here; more so than Ekman's last film, *The Marriage
Wrestler* (1964). This was also based on a play, this time a farce by Georges
Feydeau called *L'hôtel du libre échange.* It was Bergman's idea that Ekman should
make it, after the line of failures (Forslund 1982: 219), and Ekman transferred it to
a Swedish setting, Stockholm in 1912. It has a lot of energy, and Ekman's son Gösta
Ekman has a part; it was the only time he acted in one of his father's films. The
film does work well as a farce, but it is a far cry from Ekman's former glories.

   In 1964 Ekman left Sweden and moved to Spain. Since it had been the dream
of almost all his major characters since his very first films to move to South

America, it does not come as a surprise that he himself also eventually left, and if not for South America then at least to the small town of Fuengirola in the southern part of Spain. There are of course many reasons for this voluntary exile, and in a newspaper interview Ekman gave the reason that: 'it is much nicer to read a good book in Spain than bad reviews in Sweden. I am very sensitive to criticism' (Frankl 1967, trans.). When *The Marriage Wrestler* was released Ekman had already moved, after selling his art collection. The next year he was asked if he wanted to direct what was to be Sweden's first television sitcom, and he accepted. The ten episodes of *Niklasons* became a big success, and rejuvenated Swedish television (Forslund 1982: 220). That was the last time Ekman did any work with moving images, and it is both ironic and typical that the man who began his career as the filmmaker who rejuvenated Swedish cinema ended his career with rejuvenating Swedish television. It is also ironic and typical that the leading female character in *Niklasons*, played by Sickan Carlsson, in the first episode is taking Spanish lessons because she wants to be able to travel abroad, to Spain or maybe even South America.

Note

1. For theories on cinema and paintings, see for example Dalle Vacche (1996) or Felleman (2006).

CHAPTER 7
Ideas and Legacy

This book has focused on the national context but at the same time suggested that it is problematic to discuss Ekman's films as unequivocally Swedish, besides the obvious aspects of language and finance. In many of his films the nation is neither an implicit nor an explicit theme, and nationality is irrelevant for the story and for the characters. The characters are such that they could be found in most countries, as are the stories told about them. These films can be called a-national. It has been argued in earlier chapters that *With You in My Arms* could have been set in Britain and *Changing Trains* could have been set in France, but it could also be argued that *Royal Rabble* might be set in the US and *The White Cat* in Norway, to name two other possibilities. There are many other films which could have been set elsewhere. This is especially striking in the case of *The First Division*. It is about the Swedish air force but it could be any nation's air force, since it is not about the flag, or a war, but just about men in uniform under internal tensions. No countries are mentioned, which is remarkable considering the Second World War had started, and enemy aircraft might be coming from either the Soviet Union or Germany. Some of Ekman's films could have been British or French films, without changing the stories or the characters. If the same scripts had been filmed in other countries there is no reason why it would not have been possible to make the films without making any changes to the scripts or the shooting style. It is a possibility of course that they are all filled with small, telling details that would give them away for, say, a French spectator, so that s/he would not suppose that it was originally a French film, but these details are still vague and unimportant. This is one reason why it sometimes might make more sense to talk about films as regional rather than national; in Ekman's case Scandinavian or northern European. It is no coincidence that the German-American Ernst Lubitsch and the French Jean Renoir were mentioned in the introduction to this book. This is because, given his way of filmmaking, Ekman feels more international than Swedish, and his inspiration came from abroad rather than from Sweden. In an interview in 1957 Ekman said: 'My ideals were Noël Coward, Wodehouse, Capra, Lubitsch and John Ford' (Gränd 1957, trans.). He did not mention any Swedish models, not even Bauman, and in a documentary from 1993, when asked if he had had any Swedish role models or sources of influence, he said: 'From among the filmmakers, none' (Åhlund & Carlsson 1993, trans.). That Wodehouse was a model has been alluded to already, but it is hard to see anything of John Ford in Ekman's films, or of Frank Capra. There are, however, clear similarities between Ekman and Lubitsch, primarily that they both have a way of relying on visual objects and innuendos to suggest sentiments and, in particular, sexual situations. The connection with Renoir, to some extent also with Lubitsch, is a way of looking at the world rather than any thematic or stylistic influences. A thematic link exists between Lubitsch and Ekman, as mentioned earlier, in that Lubitsch's heroes have, just like Ekman's, a strong desire to rebel against and escape from the boredom of petit-bourgeois lifestyles.

Another reason why Ekman does not seem like a particularly Swedish director is that he is such an overwhelmingly urban director, compared to so many of his colleagues. Sometimes it might make sense to discuss the films as urban, rather than national or regional, and look at them together with urban films from other countries. Films that are set in the countryside might also be more easily seen as national than films set in the city, since the countryside can be more specific to a particular country than the streets of a city and also because national myths and stereotypes are more often associated with the landscape and the countryside. When Swedish films in the 1910s, 1920s and 1930s were drawing on particular national aspects, it was to a large extent the countryside – the rivers, mountains and archipelago – that was highlighted and celebrated. This is also the case with the numerous rural films and summer films that were popular in the 1940s and 1950s. Many of these films were also historical and one important aspect of national cinema is the making of historical films, films celebrating or rereading the history of a given nation. But since Ekman made films which were set in the here and now, with the exception of two films, this aspect of national cinema does not fit either when discussing his films.

However, sometimes Sweden is important in Ekman's films. It depends upon the style, content and context of the individual film, and as has been described here, some of his films are concerned with the nation, or at least aspects of Swedish society, in an explicit way. *A Day Will Come* is set during the war, but unlike *The First Division*, it is clearly about Sweden, Finland and the Soviet Union, with Swedish and Finnish soldiers fighting together to defend Finland's national integrity. So here nations are a part of the story, possibly even at the centre of it.

The Jazz Boy is a historical biopic that covers a part of Swedish history, and ends during the Second World War. Sweden here, although not a topic in itself, still becomes an important part of the story. Then there is the comedy *Little Märta Steps Forward* where the story involves a national election to the Swedish parliament. As mentioned, there is also the unofficial *folkhem* trilogy. In the first film, *Common People*, *folkhemmet* is seen as a positive force for the benefit of the working class. In the second film, *While the Door Was Locked*, the view is ambivalent, and the discussion between the old man and the caretaker, quoted in chapter 4, is especially telling. On the one hand people have received a better deal, with less poverty, for example, but on the other there is less space for individual eccentricities and life has become too regulated and orderly. In the third film, *We Three Debutantes*, the suspicion, perhaps even fear, seems to be that, despite peace and rising prosperity, the idea of *folkhemmet* that the Social Democratic Party promised, of equality and inclusiveness, has not really worked, that there are still huge class and gender differences. Another film where Sweden in itself is important is *Girl with Hyacinths*, for example in the implicit critique of Sweden's relationship with Germany during the Second World War.

Something that becomes apparent when looking at Ekman's films is that when he does engage with Sweden and Swedish society it is almost always from a critical perspective. That Ekman had an ambivalent view of Sweden is also suggested by the need his characters have to escape from it and go to South America. However, his characters are perennial potential escapees and sometimes the theatre is the goal, rather than South America. Whereas the primary reason for wanting to join the theatre is to be able to act on the stage, it is also seen as an important way out of the boredom of everyday life and the oppression of family, marriage and society. In some sense, there are similar reasons for wanting to go to South America and wanting to join the theatre, which seems to suggest that it is not necessarily Sweden that the characters want to leave behind but any kind of restrictive environment where it is not possible to be free and prosper. This of course lies at the heart of Ekman's art, and it is connected to his view of the world. It is indeed connected to his personal life, too, as Ekman dedicated his life to the theatre and cinema until he moved to Spain.

But auteurism is not just an empirical project; there is also the element of interpretation. Once the style and theme(s) of the filmmaker in question have been isolated these can then be interpreted, and an attempt to extrapolate the filmmaker's worldview can be made.

One recurring theme in Ekman's films is a sense of frustration with the way things are and a strong wish to leave a particular setting. This quote from *Wandering with the Moon* is typical of this feeling: 'I can't stand you, I can't stand myself and I can't stand my office', says the main character, Dan, to his father. This is connected to a second recurring theme: the conflict between fathers and sons, based on a conflict between the needs of the son to make something of himself, often abroad, and the father's wish for the son to follow in his footsteps. Another theme that is constantly present is the fear of, or a reaction against, the boredom and staleness of everyday life. A typical quote regarding this sentiment can be found in *With You in My Arms*, when the main character says he will change his ways and become a respectable citizen only to meet with the response: 'Oh, really? That sounds boring'. A fourth theme is an interest in outsiders, dreamers and misfits. There are many of them, who, like Dan in *Wandering with the Moon*, seek to live life on their own terms, not as followers of traditional conventions or expectations. The communist son in *The Banquet* is another example of this, as are Dagmar Brink in *Girl with Hyacinths* and Marianne Stenman in *Private Entrance*. It should also be noted, however, that Ekman occasionally problematised this wish to be free and follow nothing but one's dreams and creative needs. In a few films he showed the suffering this might cause others and how one person's dreams may be in conflict with those of another. *The White Cat* and *Knight of Hearts* are the clearest examples of this. It is one of Ekman's strengths that he acknowledges that one person's need to be free is not always a positive thing but can also be egoistic and cruel, depending upon the circumstances.

Several of Ekman's films are about the theatre, and its actors. At least eight of Ekman's films deal directly with the theatre, and other films deal with other kinds of performing arts, such as the ballet or the circus. The strong presence of artists and painters is part of his focus on misfits and dreamers, as they all have had to make the choice between real life and the life of the theatre. A fifth recurring theme is the dream of Argentina and Brazil, of South America as a continent of hope and a future. This dream recurs in almost all of Ekman's films, either as the explicit goal of a main character, or as a dream they have but are unable to realise. Finally, there is the interest in the question of identity, and the complexity of characters. This is apparent already in Ekman's first film, *With You in My Arms*. The films show how people hide their personalities or secrets, obviously in the case of all the actor-characters that appear in Ekman's films, but also many other characters. Sometimes the films also show how the mask that people assume can become their real self, and the question then becomes: What is the true nature of that self? The most puzzling example could be *Little Märta Steps Forward*, where the man, after having dressed up as a woman, starts to think and feel like a woman, and in a sense becomes a woman, and even has a statue of herself raised.

At the beginning of the book there was a quote from Ekman, something he said when he was a little boy. It is remarkable how that quote encapsulates so much of what his films are about that it bears repeating here: 'It's spooky actually. Sometimes I feel like the world is just one big theatre, and that every human being is playing a part. Some are good at it, some are bad. But we never get to read any reviews. Are you always yourself? ... I'm not, but that might not be unusual for a theatre child' (Ekman 1933: 216, trans.).

These themes are all connected with each other, and by putting them together it becomes possible to extract an idea of Ekman's view of the world. The first thing to notice, which is at the centre of that worldview, such as it can be interpreted from the actual films, is the non-negotiable importance of the individual's dignity and freedom. This can be said to be the essence of the philosophical stance of the films, although it is never stated explicitly, since neither his characters nor he himself made statements or gave speeches. This is more a case of leading by example. When all the films are taken together, with all the stories that are told and all the characters that are brought to life, that stance shines through in almost all of them. Family, marriage, conventions and society are all seen as constraints on the freedom of the individual. One of the virtues of looking at a complete body of work from an auteurist perspective is that it is often not until the combined effect of all of the films is taken into account that these larger themes emerge. Geoffrey Nowell-Smith was quoted in the first chapter as saying: 'the defining characteristics of an author's work are not always those that are most readily apparent' (Nowell-Smith 2003: 10) and this stance, this defence of the freedom and dignity of the individual, is such a defining characteristic of Ekman's oeuvre. The most horrifying attack on an individual is to be found in *His Excellency*, the anti-Nazi film in which von Blankenau is sent to a concentration camp, but these attacks on dignity and freedom also happen in peacetime, in the daily life of ordinary individuals.

There is a sequence in *While the Door Was Locked* that beautifully encapsulates the need for dignity, and how even in peacetime it is still something you might have to fight for. In the building in which the film is set live, among others, a prostitute and an old man. They both quietly go about their daily lives but at one point their paths cross. He collapses in the stairway and she picks him up and helps him to his apartment. When they enter she notices that it is completely empty, and that the floor is covered with newspapers. The old man is completely penniless, and at the end of his life, but he does not want people to know. He begs her not to tell anybody what she has seen. As long as he can keep his trousers clean and a flower in his buttonhole, he will be content. If people knew they would intervene and that would be the end of his happiness, the end of the one thing he has left in the world, his freedom and dignity. She, being a prostitute and consequently an outcast, understands him perfectly well and quietly walks out of the apartment and closes the door behind her. In so doing she allows him to keep his mask, to make it possible for him to continue playing a part and hiding his true self. There is also a political dimension involved. He would rather stay at home, and put on a brave face, than be hospitalised and taken care of by the welfare system.

The world depicted in Ekman's films is often an unpleasant one, and especially so for women. One of the factors that threaten and constrain the individual woman is patriarchal society, and as has been argued here, there is in Ekman's films a feminism than runs through his whole career. Many of his films show how both the men in themselves and the system conspire against the concerns, needs and wishes of women.

This is countered with elements of humour and parody, and sometimes an anarchic spirit. There is almost always a sense of hope, even a hope that one must fight for. This world is full of dreamers who want something else. Sometimes they aim for Brazil; sometimes they aim for the theatre. It is interesting to note, however, that, despite their being at odds with the world, there does not seem to be any kind of revolutionary instinct in the characters, other than standing up to the father. Although they suffer they are not interested in changing the system, just wanting to take care of themselves. To escape, even if escape means death, is instead the chosen path – that, or to stubbornly stick to the theatre or the studio. An exception is the communist son in *The Banquet*, but he is a very gentle rebel and he too dreams of South America. These dreamers and performers are the heroes in Ekman's films, and he views them with a combination of tenderness and frankness. It is these characters who have to fight against the stifling conventions of society.

It is important to emphasise that Ekman's films are very forgiving, in the sense that there are hardly any villains in them. The tone is non-judgemental and instead filled with sympathy. A particular character might be criticised or shown to be in the wrong, but they are often given a scene or perhaps even just one redeeming line of dialogue to add complexity. One example is Dagmar Brink's father in *Girl with Hyacinths*. He is first shown as a cruel and remorseless man, a symbol of the patriarchal system. But it is also possible to read him as a man filled with shame and guilt, who hides his feelings under a cruel mask. Gösta Cederlund, who plays him, does provide facial expressions to suggest this, and Ekman's directing underlines it, such as the way the camera lingers on him after he has been left alone. The father is also given a line which makes him more sympathetic, when he tells the story of how he saw a man shovelling snow and how he thought to himself: 'The devil knows whether you're not better off than I am'. This seems to suggest that he does not like his life or what he has become. It might be argued that while Ekman is critical of conventions and institutions, he also acknowledges that some individuals, such as Dagmar's father, are too weak to fight them, and suggests that instead of being judged they should be pitied.

With this focus on the individual and the critique of marriage, family and society, whether explicit or implicit, Ekman can be said to have been at odds with aspects of *folkhemmet*. As was explained in the first chapter, this idea, which permeated Swedish society at least until the 1960s and can be said to remain part of the Swedish psyche, albeit with a nostalgic bent, as a sense of something that has been lost, is about creating a harmonious nation-wide community in which everybody works together for the greater good. Although there is no reason to suggest that Ekman did not support the goals of *folkhemmet*, such as democracy, equality and the eradication of poverty, his films emphasise the dangers of conformity and intolerance that such a de-individualised concept can lead to. In chapter 2 Hans Ingvar Roth was quoted as arguing that there was little room for 'cultural idiosyncrasy' (Roth 2004: 222) in Sweden and this is something that Ekman was aware of and problematised in his films. That is a vital part of his work, this sustained attack against conformity. Yet, whereas Ekman does critique some aspects of Swedish society, his overarching concern is not necessarily something that is uniquely Swedish but something global. Marriage, family and the patriarchy are global phenomena, not exclusively Swedish.

As has been argued, Ekman's films are almost exclusively, and for a Swedish filmmaker uniquely, urban. One of the reasons for this is that Ekman preferred stories about people and milieus with which he himself was very familiar. This is another aspect of his auteurist credentials, that real life is closely interwoven with fictional stories in his films. He made films that had strong autobiographical elements, such as *Changing Trains*, *Royal Rabble* and *Gabrielle*, but even when they were not autobiographical they were still close to real life, especially in terms of characters, as was discussed in the previous chapter with regards to *While the Door Was Locked*, *Girl with Hyacinths* and *We Three Debutantes*. This proximity to life, this interplay between fact and fiction, is essential to Ekman's cinema. It is what makes him an internal auteur.

However, it is not only the words, the stories told and the characters' behaviour that testify to a filmmaker's worldview or philosophy. Style should also be included in the discussion. During the 1940s and early 1950s the 'battle' between Ekman and Bergman took many forms, one being that they were competing over who could shoot the longest single take. In Ekman's films, there will usually not be a cut until it is absolutely necessary. This is not only due to the competition with Bergman, but is also related to Ekman's temperament and interest. A film's philosophy, or perhaps the philosophy of the filmmaker, can be read and interpreted not only from the plot but in equal measure from how the story is told, and how editing, camera movement, colour, sound and length of shots are handled. In Ekman's case, his style underlines his outlook on life. He is an actor's director, and he stays with them as much as he can, but he does not want to intrude by going too close or by cutting away. He prefers to just watch them and see what happens. He gives space to his actors. His way of filming, frequently with long, distant takes and with relatively few close-ups, also takes on another meaning. It means that real life can intervene or interact with fiction. This can be seen primarily when the scenes take place outdoors and the environment, such as buildings and ordinary people in the background and the foreground, contribute to the mood of the shot. A particular sequence from *The Girl from the Third Row* encapsulates this approach. A woman, a fairly central character in the film, is seen running through the streets in a hurry to go to the pawnshop to get money for a trip to Italy with her lover. At one point she bumps into a man coming out of an off licence, without realising it. At another point her path is blocked by a carriage filled with celebrating students, fresh from graduation. But then, as she runs across a street, she is hit by a tram and killed. The audience do not get to see the accident, however. Ekman shoots the scene with a pan from her running to the approaching tram, and then to the face of a woman who turns her head in shock. Ekman then cuts to a curtain being pulled down at the pawnshop, followed by a shot of the man from the off licence, who is sitting on the pavement trying to

rescue the contents of the broken bottles. All through the sequence, the prevalent sound is the students singing, and depending upon where they are, their
voices are more or less audible.

What is remarkable here is that there is little sentiment, and a strong sense of
city life in all its aspects. The woman may have been killed, but the students are
cheerfully singing and the man coming from the off licence is just upset because
his bottles have been smashed. Life goes on. This, it could be argued, is an essential part of Ekman's philosophy. And this is also when it differs most distinctly
from the philosophy of Bergman, which is almost the opposite. Bergman often
presents an isolated and alienated world, in terms of both story and visuals. The
characters are cut off from the world. If Ekman's characters are within this world,
Bergman's are outside it.

In *The World Viewed* Stanley Cavell writes that:

> *Early in its history the cinema discovered the possibility of calling attention to
> persons and parts of persons and objects; but it is equally a possibility of the
> medium not to call attention to them but, rather, to let the world happen, to
> let its parts draw attention to themselves according to their natural weight.
> This possibility is less explored than its opposite. Dreyer, Flaherty, Vigo, Renoir,
> and Antonioni are masters of it.* (Cavell 1996: 163, emphasis in the original)

A case could be made for including Ekman in that category. Yet this argument
must not be pushed too hard. Not all of these directors' films are like this, and the
dichotomy is not clear-cut. It should be seen more as a general tendency than a
constant presence. What this approach, 'to let the world happen', does, though,
at least in the case of Ekman, is to help put things in the right perspective, the
perspective Ekman often felt was missing in Bergman. As was suggested earlier, in
Ekman's films there is a sense of a world outside the frame. The single individuals
are not really that important in the bigger picture; the world goes on regardless of
their petty affairs. Bergman's cinema is a cinema of the closed room – a few characters in a secluded environment – whereas Ekman's is the cinema of the open
door. The story that is told is just one of many possible stories, and the world is
bigger than any of the characters in the film. This sense of intermingling real life
and fiction also comes across in Ekman's style of filming, the way that the films are
often shot out on location, rather than in the studio, and how, even when scenes
are shot in a studio, efforts are made to make it feel as real as possible. This fits

with Ekman's shooting style, where the camera remains at a distance from the actors, whereas Bergman's work is famous for its close-ups. Ekman's use of loose narratives, sometimes of an episodic nature, is also relevant here as it is closer to actual life, giving more breathing space than a focused, narrow narrative would do. *Wandering with the Moon* is a prime example of this. The way Ekman usually ends his films, by a repetition of the first scene with an important difference, is also an important factor for this argument. As was said about both *Changing Trains* and *The Girl from the Third Row*, the very narrative construction of some of his films has the audience vacillating between the themes of hope and despair, love and betrayal, and life and death. The visual style, the narrative structure and the world-view become inseparable.

It is also the case that some auteurs, within the framework of their particular themes and motifs, subtly change, modify and question these themes. An artist can keep his or her main concerns but look at them from different angles. This might make the body of work richer, as it suggests a more complex and nuanced understanding of the world than might be implied from only one or two films. This is the case with Ekman: in two films made in 1950, *Knight of Hearts* and *The White Cat*, the solitary, creative and life-affirming characters, who are usually the heroes for Ekman, are shown to be cruel and exploitative.

After this discussion of Ekman's themes and style one thing remains, and that is to consider what kind of impact he had on Swedish cinema, and to what extent he influenced other filmmakers. Influence is complex. Sometimes an artist may do something that appears to be influenced by a previous artist, even though s/he is not aware of the work of that artist. Similarities do not in themselves signify influences. It can be more about the spirit of the times than a question of one person necessarily influencing another. One can also talk about similarities between filmmakers based on similar approaches to filmmaking and to life in general, without there being any actual influence of one on the other. Any similarities between Renoir and Ekman should be taken as an example of this, a shared outlook on life and perspective on the characters, rather than the one being overtly influenced by the other. With Lubitsch it is a combination of Ekman being more directly influenced by him as well as sharing some of his views on life and people.

Nevertheless, this section will look at Ekman's impact on Swedish cinema. There are two different aspects to this. The first is how Ekman's films and film-making made a difference and added something new to Swedish cinema, partly because Ekman's inspiration was more to be found in France, Britain and Hollywood than in traditional Swedish cinema. It is reasonable to say that Ekman was a cinephile, a filmmaker who was in love with cinema and who watched as many films as he could find the time for, not least on his trip to Hollywood, which was mentioned in chapter 4. Because of this it can be said that he brought a new approach to Swedish filmmaking, a professionalism and cinematic know-how combined with a relaxed attitude to rules and conventions. When his first film appeared, the critics said that it was like a breath of fresh air, and this is primarily related to the style of filmmaking and directing actors. It can be argued that another thing he popularised was a deeply personal cinema. Although it was not unheard of before, the extent to which Ekman made films about himself and his life was definitely not common in Swedish cinema at the time, and neither was the way he would include scenes in his films which were discussions of his own private fears and relationships. He also introduced and/or developed several important actors and actresses: Stig Järrel, Gunnar Björnstrand and Eva Henning were among them. And he was one of the very first Swedish filmmakers who had a stock company; a select group of actors who would be used in film after film. It was how Bergman would later work as well.

The second aspect is the importance of Ekman as a writer and actor. He wrote scripts for a number of other filmmakers, and he acted in many films other than those he himself directed. It might be said that he was what is today called a 'script doctor', somebody that is called in when there are problems with a script. With his skills and popularity he helped many careers besides his own. Arne Mattsson, Schamyl Bauman, Rolf Husberg and Gustaf Molander are among those directors he worked with and wrote for.

These two aspects then coalesce in the particular case of Ingmar Bergman. The characteristics that it can reasonably be argued Ekman brought to Swedish cinema were picked up by Bergman. Bergman would also make deeply personal films, and he would have a stock company of actors, several of whom had begun working with Ekman. Since the two of them were working closely together, albeit competing, Bergman was in a position to learn a lot from Ekman, and vice versa.

In the late 1960s, Bergman would go further than Ekman when it came to pushing the film medium forward through narrative and visual inventiveness, in films such as *Persona* (1966) and *The Hour of the Wolf* (*Vargtimmen*, 1968). In addition, Bergman and the new filmmakers of the 1960s began making films that were more explicit about sex and violence than Ekman's had ever been. Other than that, much of what was considered new and revolutionary in the 1960s had often been done by Ekman in the 1940s and early 1950s, such as critical engagement with society, self-reflexiveness, experiments with narrative and a commitment to emotional honesty. That is not to say that the 1960s filmmakers were influenced by Ekman, although some of them might have been. It is just to point out that Ekman was a modern and often daring filmmaker.

And it is this influence, this modern and personal approach to filmmaking and the high and persistent quality of his films that make it possible to argue that Ekman should be regarded as not only one of the most important filmmakers Sweden has ever had, but also a major artist in the history of European cinema. It should be remembered that Henri Langlois was running regular screenings of world cinema at the Cinémathèque Française in Paris after the Second World War and that the future filmmakers of the French New Wave, such as Eric Rohmer, François Truffaut and Jean-Luc Godard, were there, watching these films. Many of these films were Swedish, and the influence Bergman had on the French New Wave is often mentioned by both film historians and the filmmakers themselves, but in all likelihood they also watched films by Ekman. It is not far-fetched to imagine that Truffaut both watched and liked the films by Ekman, and was perhaps inspired by them. In an article about Ekman in 1985, the leading Swedish critic Leif Zern describes Ekman as 'a Swedish Truffaut', not least for the way he 'overwhelmingly combines tragedy and humour' (Zern 1985, trans.). But since Ekman came before Truffaut maybe it would be more apt to say that Truffaut was 'a French Ekman'.

This book has discussed Ekman from the perspective of authorship and national context but there are many other approaches which were not possible to incorporate here but that can be used for further research into his films. To further explore the possible connections between Ekman and the French filmmakers mentioned above is an approach which might lead to interesting revelations. Another approach would be to analyse Ekman's work with actors, and how he and Bergman and other directors differed in the way they used their actors. This would be especially interesting since many of the actors, such as Gunnar Björnstrand, played prominent roles in the work of several filmmakers. Another approach could be to look at Ekman's films in terms of theories of urbanity and cinema and the city. This is a growing field within film studies and since Ekman is such an urban filmmaker he is a valuable case study. Yet another approach that might lead to interesting insights would be to look at his body of work from the perspective of queer theory. With his interest in role playing, cross-dressing and, of course, the central role *Girl with Hyacinths* has in his oeuvre, Ekman would be a good case study here too. With such a large, complex and rich body of work as that of Hasse Ekman it is not possible to cover everything in one book. The hope is that this work will be seen as an important and comprehensive study which can be used as a foundation for further research.

Conclusion

Swedish cinema has traditionally been held in high regard, and its history has to some extent been well documented. However, there are still some gaps in the study of Swedish film history. The first gap concerns Swedish cinema of the 1940s and the second gap concerns the filmmaker Hasse Ekman. This era and this film-maker were chosen for this study because they are important for Swedish cinema and should be discussed and analysed. Considering the influence and status of Swedish cinema internationally, conducting research on the 1940s and Hasse Ekman is also important from a global perspective. So in this study Ekman's work has been analysed in terms of recurring stylistic and thematic motifs, and it has been argued that he was an auteur, although his relationship to the social and cinematic context in which he worked is also important. The discussion has also touched on the often fraught relationship between Ekman and Ingmar Bergman, the auteur who, more than any other, to critics and scholars has come to embody the importance of post-war Swedish cinema.

It is widely reckoned that it was in the 1950s, following the crucial critical inter-vention of the French journal *Cahiers du cinéma*, that the director became the focus of aesthetic attention. However, at least from the 1910s it has been custom-ary to single out the director as the most important person in the making of a film, both among critics and in the film industry itself, and some leading theorists in the 1920s called the director the author of the film. Authorship studies have been a central part of cinema studies ever since, and continues to be a relevant emphasis in the study of film history, using an approach which has come to be called auteur-ism. It is not a theory but a critical approach, or methodological focus, which is empirical. In addition, a distinction has been made here between *external* and *internal* auteurs. An external auteur is a filmmaker whose films have the thematic and stylistic consistency of an auteur but the filmmaker him/herself has no pres-ence in the films. An internal auteur is a figure who has a strong personal presence in the films, for example by acting in them and/or doing voice-overs, or by making autobiographical films. Hasse Ekman can be seen as an internal auteur.

But no auteur has worked in a vacuum: the context is important too, and here that context is Sweden. All of Ekman's films were made in Sweden (including two international projects), and although some of Ekman's films have themes and characters that are not specific to any one nation and can be called 'a-national', some do discuss, and directly engage with, specific Swedish topics and concerns.

The silent era, particularly in the years 1913 to 1924, is considered something of a golden age of Swedish cinema, when filmmakers such as Victor Sjöström, Mauritz Stiller and Georg af Klercker were active. After several years of problems, both financial and artistic, in 1940 Swedish films experienced a renaissance that lasted approximately until 1953. Hasse Ekman was a leading figure in this renaissance, as actor, writer and director, and among other notable filmmakers of this renaissance Alf Sjöberg, Per Lindberg, Hampe Faustman, Arne Sucksdorff, Olof Molander, Gustaf Molander and Ingmar Bergman should be mentioned. Some had made one or two films before, but most began their careers in the 1940s. One reason for this creative outburst was the Second World War when there was a large and eager audience in Sweden, and they wanted to see Swedish films. This wish, combined with fewer foreign films coming to Sweden owing to wartime restrictions, meant that it was very profitable to make films, and producers were willing to let filmmakers experiment both visually and with narrative, and make films about important and difficult subjects. At the same time, film societies sprang up and leading newspapers and cultural journals began writing informed criticism and essays about cinema.

But by the early 1950s the audience began to lose interest in Swedish films, and at the same time producers and production companies had to struggle with rising taxes and production costs. The most serious problem, however, was the arrival of television in 1956, which led to an almost immediate collapse in box-office figures. The result was that fewer films were made and there was much less scope for artistically challenging and experimental work.

Hasse Ekman's career followed this broader trajectory for Swedish cinema. He made his first film, *With You in My Arms*, in 1940, the same year the Swedish renaissance can be said to have begun, and he made the film which is often considered to be his last great one, *Gabrielle*, in 1954, shortly after the renaissance had passed. In 1956, when television emerged, his career took another turn as he made a series of colourful comedies (whereas before he had mainly made sombre dramas), until he lost interest in filmmaking. He made his last film in 1964 before moving to Spain. Whilst there were turning points in Ekman's career, there is a strong consistency in his oeuvre from 1940 until his final films.

The characters in Ekman's films share certain traits; among them is a fundamental feeling of not fitting in and of being constrained. Whether from marriage, family, work or society at large, his characters have a strong need to escape, and there are primarily two escape routes for them. One is into the theatre or other art forms such as painting, and the other is to go abroad, especially to South America. Besides the constraints of rules and traditions, what also troubles his characters is the boredom and stagnation that arise from daily routine, something that art or the larger world can perhaps remedy. Another strong, recurring motif in Ekman's films is play-acting and people who are confused about their own identities or are hiding their true identities from the rest of the world. This appears in the many films he has made that are set in the theatre and are about actors and acting, but even outside the theatre these games are played out. Often when people pretend, and hide their secrets, it is because they want to protect their dignity, especially if they are sick or poor, or living in shame.

Ekman's view of society can be bleak but the heroes of his films are those that fight for their freedom and dignity. This is especially so for women, and there is a feminist side to Ekman's films as he has created many strong, independent female characters who struggle in a society dominated by men.

One reason why Ekman can be called an internal auteur is because he acts in almost all of his films, and there is an interesting relationship between his characters, himself and his public persona. Some of the films are also autobiographical, more or less explicitly so, and this is especially the case with those that are set in the theatre, such as *Changing Trains* or *Royal Rabble*. Ekman also used his films to discuss personal concerns, such as questions about art, family and relationships. Some of his films were mere assignments, but even in those few films that he made because he was obliged to, rather than because he had a particular story to tell, these specific characters and themes that are typical of Ekman still appear. Something that is also distinct about Ekman, and that makes him different from almost all other Swedish filmmakers of the time, is that his films are distinctly urban, almost exclusively set in the city. Rural dramas, 'summer films' and films set in the archipelago were traditionally very popular in Sweden, and most filmmakers, including Bergman, made such films. But not Ekman. Sweden outside Stockholm hardly figures at all, and when it does it is a transitory space. *First Division* is set in the north of Sweden and *Country House Wanted* is partly set in the archipelago, but only *Wandering with the Moon* takes place completely in the countryside.

Stylistically, Ekman favours long takes and deep focus, but he is more interested in the actors than in pictorialism. His takes are sometimes complex, following characters as they move around, in order not to break up the scene but instead let the actors remain in focus. Sometimes his films have surrealist sequences, such as nightmares or, in the later films, dance sequences, but on the whole he aims for realism, in that the films are set in this world, with geographical locations often highlighted by a voice-over or with signs. Much is filmed on location, particularly on the streets of Stockholm, to emphasis this sense of the world.

During the 1940s, Ekman was frequently described by the critics as Sweden's best filmmaker but when Ingmar Bergman made his first film in 1945 there was almost immediately competition between them. The critics began to compare them, and each year when the award for best Swedish film was handed out it was given to either a film by Ekman or a film by Bergman. They were also competing personally, for example over the longest take. In 1949 Bergman made *Prison*, and later the same year Ekman made what he himself called an 'anti-Bergman film', *The Girl from the Third Row*. The two films are similar in their complex structures, but Ekman's film is a protest against the relentless hopelessness of Bergman's film. Ekman's film acknowledges that life is filled with hardship and suffering, but it suggests that hope and love also exist, that there is a sort of balance.

The competition between the two filmmakers lasted until 1956, when Ekman gave up the ambition to make serious and challenging films, and instead made a series of comedies. But he did also make one or two films of a more serious nature, and the later films still had typical Ekman themes, extending even to the television series *Niklasons*. This was the last work Ekman directed for either film or television, and he had by then moved to Spain, where he would remain for the rest of his life.

Besides making films of high quality, Ekman's importance lies primarily in breathing new life into Swedish cinema. This was partly through his own professionalism and creativity and partly because he was inspired by French and US cinema, rather than Swedish. The fact that, as a writer and director, he made films that were often based on his own life was also important as this was relatively rare for Swedish cinema at the time. For these reasons, Ekman played a central role in the 1940s renaissance of Swedish cinema, and this is why his work is so significant.

There is a need to look at Swedish cinema from a new perspective, and it is appropriate to consider Hasse Ekman as an auteur – more to the point, an internal auteur – and a filmmaker with important themes and considerable skill. But the work of discussing and analysing Swedish cinema and Ekman, as well as film history in general, will continue. If audiences can learn anything from Ekman it is the need to go against conventions and complacency, to be creative as well as playful. Film history is not fixed and stable: it changes all the time. The importance once given to particular films, filmmakers and movements is not set in stone, and is partly dependent on the interests and priorities of film historians and scholars at any given time. At the same time, many films and filmmakers are forgotten, misunderstood or under-appreciated. The hope is that by now the reader's perspective on Swedish cinema and on Bergman has changed, besides their having been introduced to the world of Hasse Ekman.

Filmography

In the following lists, nationality is only mentioned for non-Swedish titles.

Films Written by Hasse Ekman

Thunder and Lightning (*Blixt och dunder*, Anders Henriksson, 1938)

Heroes in Yellow and Blue (*Hjältar i gult och blått*, Schamyl Bauman, 1940)

A Man in Full (*Karl för sin hatt*, Schamyl Bauman, 1940)

Swing It, Teacher! (*'Swing it' magistern!*, Schamyl Bauman, 1940)

Men of the Navy (*Örlogsmän*, Börje Larsson, 1943)

Life and Death (*På liv och död*, Rolf Husberg, 1943)

Love and Downhill Racing (*Kärlek och störtlopp*, Rolf Husberg, 1946)

The Kiss on the Cruise (*Kyssen på kryssen*, Arne Mattsson, 1950)

Journey to You (*Resan till dej*, Stig Olin, 1953)

Films Directed by Hasse Ekman

With You in My Arms (*Med dej i mina armar*, 1940)

The First Division (*Första divisionen*, 1941)

Happiness Approaches (*Lyckan kommer*, 1942)

Flames in the Dark (*Lågor i dunklet*, 1942)

The Sixth Shot (*Det sjätte skottet*, 1943)

Changing Trains (*Ombyte av tåg*, 1943)

Common People (*Som folk är mest*, 1944)

His Excellency (*Excellensen*, 1944)

An Occupation for Men (*Ett yrke för män*, 1944)

A Day Will Come (*En dag skall gry*, 1944)

Wandering with the Moon (*Vandring med månen*, 1945)

Royal Rabble (*Kungliga patrasket*, 1945)

Little Märta Steps Forward (*Fram för lilla Märta*, 1945)

Meeting in the Night (*Möte i natten*, 1946)

While the Door Was Locked (*Medan porten var stängd*, 1946)

Waiting Room for Death aka Interlude (*I dödens väntrum*, 1946)

One Swallow Does Not Make a Summer (*En fluga gör ingen sommar*, 1947)

To Each His Own (*Var sin väg*, 1948)

The Return of Little Märta (*Lilla Märta kommer tillbaka*, 1948)

The Banquet (*Banketten*, 1948)

The Girl from the Third Row (*Flickan från tredje raden*, 1949)

Girl with Hyacinths (*Flicka och hyacinter*, 1950)

Knight of Hearts (*Hjärter knekt*, 1950)

The White Cat (*Den vita katten*, 1950)

House of Madness (*Dårskapens hus*, 1951)

The Fire-Bird (*Eldfågeln*, 1952)

We Three Debutantes (*Vi tre debutera*, 1953)

Gabrielle (1954)

Private Entrance (*Egen ingång*, 1956)

Seventh Heaven (*Sjunde himlen*, 1956)

Ratataa or The Staffan Stolle Story (1956)

Country House Wanted (*Sommarnöje sökes*, 1957)

The Halo is Slipping (*Med glorian på sned*, 1957)

The Jazz Boy (*Jazzgossen*, 1958)

The Great Amateur (*Den stora amatören*, 1958)

Great Scott! (*Himmel och pannkaka*, 1959)

Miss Chic (*Fröken Chic*, 1959)

On a Bench in a Park (*På en bänk i en park*, 1960)

Decimals of Love (*Kärlekens decimaler*, 1960)

The Heist (*Stöten*, 1961)

My Love is Like a Rose (*Min kära är en ros*, 1963)

The Marriage Wrestler (Äktenskapsbrottaren, 1964)

Niklasons (1965 television series)

Other Films

In the following list, titles in which Ekman appears as an actor are marked 'HE'.

Adam's Rib (George Cukor, 1949, USA)

...And All These Women (... och alla dessa kvinnor, Arne Mattsson, 1944)

Appassionata (Olof Molander, 1944)

Artificial Svensson (Konstgjorda Svensson, Gustav Edgren, 1929)

Bachelor Mother (Garson Kanin, 1939, USA)

Battle Goes On, The (Striden går vidare, Gustaf Molander, 1941)

Ben-Hur: A Tale of the Christ (Fred Niblo, 1925, USA)

Beyond a Reasonable Doubt (Fritz Lang, 1956, USA)

Blue Dahlia, The (George Marshall, 1946, USA)

Born Yesterday (George Cukor, 1950, USA)

Boudu Saved from Drowning (Boudu sauvé des eaux, Jean Renoir, 1932, France)

Bread of Love, The (Kärlekens bröd, Arne Mattsson, 1953)

Career (Karriär, Schamyl Bauman, 1938)

Casablanca (Michael Curtiz, 1942, USA)

Christine (Un carnet de bal, Julien Duvivier, 1937, France)

Citizen Kane (Orson Welles, 1941, USA)

Crime, A (Ett brott, Anders Henriksson, 1940)

Crime of Monsieur Lange, The (Le crime de M. Lange, Jean Renoir, 1935, France)

Crisis (Kris, Ingmar Bergman, 1946)

Design for Living (Ernst Lubitsch, 1933, USA)

Double Indemnity (Billy Wilder, 1944, USA)

Dream Waltz, The (Säg det i toner, Edvin Adolphson, Julius Jaenzon, 1929)

Emigrants, The (Utvandrarna, Jan Troell, 1971)

Foreign Harbour (Främmande hamn, Erik Hampe Faustman, 1948)

For Her Sake (*För hennes skull*, Paul Merzbach, 1930)

French Provincial (*Souvenirs d'en France*, André Téchiné, 1975, France)

Girls in Småland, The (*Flickorna i Småland*, Schamyl Bauman, 1945)

Grande Illusion, La (Jean Renoir, 1937, France)

Great Adventure, The (*Det stora äventyret*, Arne Sucksdorff, 1953)

Heavenly Play, The (*Himlaspelet*, Alf Sjöberg, 1942)

Home from Babylon (*Hem från Babylon*, Alf Sjöberg, 1941)

Hôtel du Nord (Marcel Carné, 1938, France)

Hour of the Wolf, The (*Vargtimmen*, Ingmar Bergman, 1968)

Imprisoned Women (*Kvinnor i fångenskap*, Olof Molander, 1943)

In Darkest Småland (*I mörkaste Småland*, Schamyl Bauman, 1943)

Indian Village, An (*Indisk by*, Arne Sucksdorff, 1951)

Intermezzo (Gustaf Molander, 1936)

Intolerance (D.W. Griffith, 1916, USA)

It Rains on Our Love (*Det regnar på vår kärlek*, Ingmar Bergman, 1946)

Karl Fredrik Reigns (*Karl Fredrik regerar*, Gustaf Edgren, 1934)

Kon-tiki (Thor Heyerdahl, 1950, Norway, Sweden)

Lars Hård (Erik Hampe Faustman, 1948)

Little Flirt, A (*En stilla flirt*, Gustaf Molander, 1934)

Living on 'Hope' (*Leva på 'Hoppet'*, Göran Gentele, 1951)

Lydia (Julien Duvivier, 1941, USA)

Miracle in Milan (*Miracolo a Milano*, Vittorio de Sica, 1951, Italy)

Miss Julie (*Fröken Julie*, Alf Sjöberg, 1951)

Night in Harbour (*Natt i hamn*, Erik Hampe Faustman, 1943)

Night Must Fall (Richard Thorpe, 1937, USA)

One Night (*En natt*, Gustaf Molander, 1931)

One Summer of Happiness (*Hon dansade en sommar*, Arne Mattsson, 1951)

Only a Mother (*Bara en mor*, Alf Sjöberg, 1949)

Persona (Ingmar Bergman, 1966)

Pettersson & Bendel (Per-Axel Branner, 1933)

Phantom Carriage, The (Körkarlen, Victor Sjöström, 1921)

Port of Shadows (Quai de brumes, Marcel Carné, 1938, France)

Pram, The (Barnvagnen, Bo Widerberg, 1963)

Prison aka *The Devil's Wanton (Fängelse,* Ingmar Bergman, 1949) HE

Red Day, The (Röda dagen, Gustaf Edgren, 1931)

Red Shoes, The (Michael Powell, 1948, UK)

Rejoice While You're Young, Fellow Cadets (Gläd dig i din ungdom, Per Lindberg, 1939)

Romance (Romans, Åke Ohberg, 1940)

Rospiggar (Schamyl Bauman, 1942)

Rules of the Game, The (La règle du jeu, Jean Renoir, 1939, France)

Salka Valka (Arne Mattsson, 1954)

Sawdust and Tinsel (Gycklarnas afton, Ingmar Bergman, 1953) HE

Seventh Seal, The (Det sjunde inseglet, Ingmar Bergman, 1957)

Ship to India, A (Skepp till Indialand, Ingmar Bergman, 1947)

Shop Around the Corner, The (Ernst Lubitsch, 1940, USA)

Smiles of a Summer Night (Sommarnattens leende, Ingmar Bergman, 1955)

Steel (Stål, Per Lindberg, 1940)

Stimulantia (Jörn Donner, Lars Görling, Ingmar Bergman, Arne Arnbom, Hans Alfredson, Tage Danielsson, Gustaf Molander, Vilgot Sjöman, Hans Abrahamson, 1967)

Stop! Think about Something Else (Stopp! Tänk på något annat, Åke Ohberg, 1944) HE

Summer Interlude (Sommarlek, Ingmar Bergman, 1951)

Summer with Monika (Sommaren med Monika, Ingmar Bergman, 1953)

Sunshine Follows Rain (Driver dagg, faller regn, Gustaf Edgren, 1946)

Sussie (Arne Mattsson, 1945)

Swedenhielms Family (Swedenhielms, Gustaf Molander, 1935)

Symphony of a City (Människor i stad, Arne Sucksdorff, 1947)

Tales of Manhattan (Julien Duvivier, 1942, USA)

They Staked Their Lives (Med livet som insats, Alf Sjöberg, 1940)

Thirst aka *Three Strange Loves* (*Törst*, Ingmar Bergman, 1949) HE

Tom, Dick and Harry (Garson Kanin, 1941, USA)

Torment aka *Frenzy* (*Hets*, Alf Sjöberg, 1944)

Towards a New Dawn (*Mot nya tider*, Sigurd Wallén, 1939)

Two of Us, The (*Vi två*, Schamyl Bauman, 1939)

Tyranny of Hate, The (*Bodakungen*, Gustaf Molander, 1920)

Vagabond Blacksmiths (*Smeder på luffen*, Erik Hampe Faustman, 1949)

Wages of Fear, The (*Le salaire de la peur*, Henri-Georges Clouzot, 1953, France)

Wanted (*Efterlyst*, Schamyl Bauman, 1939)

When Roses Bloom (*När rosorna slå ut*, Edvin Adolphson, 1930)

When the Meadows Are in Bloom (*När ängarna blomma*, Erik Hampe Faustman, 1946)

While the City Sleeps (*Medan staden sover*, Lars-Eric Kjellgren, 1950)

Wild Strawberries (*Smultronstället*, Ingmar Bergman, 1957)

Witches' Night (*Häxnatten*, Schamyl Bauman, 1937)

With the People for the Motherland (*Med folket för fosterlandet*, Sigurd Wallén, 1938)

Woman in the Window, The (Fritz Lang, 1944, USA)

Woman's Face, A (*En kvinnas ansikte*, Gustaf Molander, 1938)

Young Nobleman, The (*Unga greven tar flickan och priset*, Rune Carlsten, 1924) HE

Television

Bonanza (1959–1973, USA)

Forsyte Saga, The (1967, UK)

Hylands hörna (Hyland's Corner, 1962–1983)

Kvitt eller dubbelt (All or Nothing, 1957-1961)

The $64 000 Question (1955-1958, USA)

The Tonight Show Starring Johnny Carson (1962–1992, USA)

List of Works Cited

A.G.B. 1949. Review of *The Girl from the Third Row*, *Aftontidningen*, 30 August, no page. Hasse Ekman Archives.

Agrell, W. 2004. 'In the Innermost Sanctum: Reflections on the Mythology of Sweden's Neutrality Policy and the History of Questioning', in K. Almqvist and K. Glans (eds), *The Swedish Success Story?* trans. P. Fischer. Stockholm: Axel and Margaret Ax:son Johnson Foundation, pp. 187–197.

Åhlund, J. and G. Carlsson. 1993. *Möte med Hasse*. Documentary produced by Göteborg International Film Festival.

Alm, M. 2009. 'Bilden av Amerika', in J. Christensson (ed.), *Signums svenska kulturhistoria 1900-tal*. Lund: Signum, pp. 179–197.

Almqvist, S. 1945. Review of *With You in My Arms*, *Aftontidningen*, 20 January, no page. Hasse Ekman Archives.

Andersson, K.-O. 1995. *Vårt dramatiska sekel – beredskapsår och efterkrigstid*. Stockholm: Brevskolan.

Axelsson, C. 1995. 'Bergman vs. Ekman', *Filmrutan* 4, pp. 16–21.

Bang. 1945. Review of *Lilla Märta Steps Forward*, *Dagens Nyheter*, 30 September, no page. Hasse Ekman Archives.

Barthes, R. 1977. 'The Death of the Author', in *Image – Music – Text*, trans. S. Heath. London: Fontana, pp. 142–149.

_____. 1994. *Roland Barthes by Roland Barthes*, trans. R. Howard. Berkeley: University of California Press.

Bergenheim, Å. 2009. 'Sexualdebattens århundrade', in J. Christensson (ed.), *Signums svenska kulturhistoria 1900-tal*. Lund: Signum, pp. 117–137.

Bergman, I. 1995. *Images: My Life in Film*, trans. M. Ruuth. London: Faber & Faber.

Beyer, N. 1951. 'Hasse Ekmans skandalfilm', *Morgon-Tidningen*, 13 October, no page. Hasse Ekman Archives.

Björck, H. 2008. *Folkhemsbyggare*. Stockholm: Atlantis.

_____. 2009. 'Ingenjörerna', in J. Christensson (ed.), *Signums svenska kulturhistoria 1900-tal*. Lund: Signum, pp. 331–355.

Björkman, C. 1949. Review of *The Girl from the Third Row*, *Dagens Nyheter*, 30 August, no page. Hasse Ekman Archives.

_____. 1950. Review of *The White Cat*, *Dagens Nyheter*, 19 September, no page. Hasse Ekman Archives.

_____. 1954. Review of *Gabrielle*, *Dagens Nyheter*, 27 December, no page. Hasse Ekman Archives.

_____. 1956. Review of *Seventh Heaven*, *Dagens Nyheter*, 12 June, no page. Hasse Ekman Archives.

_____. 1960. Review of *Decimals of Love*, *Dagens Nyheter*, 12 September, no page. Hasse Ekman Archives.

Björkman, S., T. Manns and J. Sima (eds). 1993. *Bergman on Bergman*. New York: Simon & Schuster.

Bordwell, D. 1985. *Narration in the Fiction Film*. London: Methuen & Co Ltd.

Bordwell, D. and K. Thompson. 2003. *Film History – An Introduction*, 2nd ed. New York: McGraw-Hill.

Calvet, L.-J. 1994. *Roland Barthes: A Biography*, trans. S. Wykes. Cambridge: Polity Press.

Cavell, S. 1996. *The Cavell Reader*, ed. S. Mulhall. Cambridge: Blackwell.

Childs, M.W. 1944. *Sweden: The Middle Way*. New Haven: Yale University Press.

Coates, P. 1985. *The Story of the Lost Reflection: The Alienation of the Image in Western and Polish Cinema*. London: Verso.

Cook, D.A. 2004. *A History of Narrative Film*, 4th ed. New York: W.W. Norton & Company.

Corrigan, T. and P. White (eds). 2009. *The Film Experience – An Introduction*, 2nd ed. Boston: Bedford/St Martin's.

Cousins, M. 2004. *The Story of Film*. London: Pavilion Books.

Cowie, P. 1985. *Swedish Cinema, from Ingeborg Holm to Fanny and Alexander*. Stockholm: Swedish Institute.

Dahlberg, H. 1999. *Hundra år i Sverige*. Stockholm: Albert Bonnier.

Dalle Vacche, A. 1996. *Cinema and Painting – How Art is Used in Film*. London: The Athlone Press.

DeAngelis, M. 2006. 'Authorship and New Queer Cinema: The Case of Todd Haynes', in B.K. Grant (ed.), *Auteurs and Authorship – A Film Reader* (2008). Malden: Blackwell Publishing.

Ekman, H. 1933. *Hur ska det gå för mig?* Stockholm: Lars Hökerbergs bokförlag.

_____. 1938. 'Min älskade pappa', in G. Tranströmer (ed.), *Minnesboken – Gösta Ekman Människan och konstnären*. Stockholm: Åhlen och Åkerlund, pp. 4–7.

_____. 1955. *Den vackra ankungen*. Stockholm: Wahlström & Widstrand.

E.L. 1959. Review of *Miss Chic*, *Ny Dag*, 27 January, no page. Hasse Ekman Archives.

Epstein, J. 1988. 'On Certain Characteristics of *Photogénie*', in R. Abel (ed.), *French Film Theory and Criticism – A History/Anthology 1907–1939*. Princeton: Princeton University Press, pp. 314–318.

Eyman, S. 1993. *Ernst Lubitsch: Laughter in Paradise*. New York: Simon & Schuster.

Felleman, S. 2006. *Art in the Cinematic Imagination*. Austin: University of Texas Press.

Forslund, B. 1982. *Från Gösta Ekman till Gösta Ekman – en bok om Hasse, far och son*. Stockholm: Askild & Kärnekull Förlag AB.

_____. 2003. *Molander – Molander – Molander*. Stockholm: Carlsson.

Foucault, M. 1977. 'What is an Author?' in D.F. Bouchard (ed.), *Language – Counter-Memory – Practice*, trans. D.F. Bouchard and S. Simon. Oxford: Basil Blackwell, pp. 113–138.

Frankl, E. 1967. 'Har du misslyckats som konstnär Hasse Ekman?' *Aftonbladet*, 10 December, no page. Hasse Ekman Archives.

Furhammar, L. 1991. *Filmen i Sverige*. Höganäs: Förlags AB Wiken.

Furhammar, L. and J. Åhlund. 1993. *En liten bok om Hasse*. Göteborg: Filmkonst.

Gervais, M. 1999. *Ingmar Bergman: Magician and Prophet*. Montreal: McGill-Queen's University Press.

Gränd, S. 1957. 'Mellan film 34 och 35', *Bildjournalen* 11, no page. Hasse Ekman Archives.

Grant, G. 2000. 'www.auteur.com?' *Screen* 41, 1, pp. 101–108.

Grodal, T. 2004. 'Agency in Film, Filmmaking, and Reception', in T. Grodal, B. Larsen and I. Thorving Laursen (eds), *Visual Authorship: Creativity and Intentionality in Media*. Copenhagen: Museum Tusculanums Press, pp. 15–36.

Gustafsson, F. 2007. *Ture Nerman – en ideologisk resa*. Masters dissertation. Stockholm: Stockholms Universitet.

Habel, Y. 2002. *Modern Media, Modern Audience: Mass Media and Social Engineering in the 1930s Swedish Welfare State*. Stockholm: Aura.

Hadenius, S. 2003. *Modern svensk politisk historia – konflikt och samförstånd*, 6th ed. Stockholm: Hjalmarsson och Högberg.

Heath, S. 1973. 'Comments on "The Idea of Authorship"', *Screen* 14, 3, pp. 86–91.

Heed, B. 1950. '*Flicka och hyacinter*. Varannan biobesökare fattar ej slutet', *Aftonbladet*, 19 March, no page. Microfilm, Swedish Film Institute.

Higson, A. 1995. *Waving the Flag: Constructing a National Cinema in Britain*. Oxford: Clarendon Press.

Hirdman, Y. 2010. *Att lägga livet tillrätta*, 3rd ed. Stockholm: Carlsson.

Hjort, M. and U. Lindqvist (eds.). 2016. *A Companion to Nordic Cinema*. Malden, Wiley-Blackwell.

Hofsten, E. and H. Lundström. 1976. *Swedish Population History Main Trends from 1750–1970*. Stockholm: Liber.

Höken. 1961. Review of *The Heist*, *Svenska Dagbladet*, 5 September, no page. Hasse Ekman Archives.

Hollows, J. and M. Jancovich (eds). 1995. *Approaches to Popular Film*. Manchester: Manchester University Press.

Hood, R. 1945. Review of *Wandering with the Moon*, *Stockholms Tidningen*, 7 August, no page. Hasse Ekman Archives.

_____. 1946. Review of *While the Door Was Locked*, *Stockholms Tidningen*, 27 December, no page. Hasse Ekman Archives.

_____. 1950. 'Filmskott', *Stockholms Tidningen*, 12 March, no page. Microfilm, Swedish Film Institute.

_____. 1951. Untitled, *Stockholms Tidningen*, 5 February, no page. Microfilm, Swedish Film Institute.

Horton, A. (ed.). 1997. *The Last Modernist: The Films of Theo Angelopoulos*. Trowbridge: Flicks Books.

Johnston, C. (ed.). 1975. *The Work of Dorothy Arzner: Towards a Feminist Cinema*. London, British Film Institute.

Kael, P. 2007. 'Circles and Squares', in *I Lost it at the Movies: Film Writings 1954 to 1965*, 4th ed. New York: Marion Boyars, pp. 292–319.

Karlsson, Y. 2000. 'Filmmysterium utlöste tidig debatt om homosexualitet. "Flickor på ängen" viktig pusselbit', *Läkartidningen* 13, pp. 1,568–1,569.

Kindblom, M. 2004. 'Mannen som älskade film', *Ordfront* 3, pp. 40–46.

_____. 2006. *Våra drömmars stad – Stockholm i filmen*. Stockholm: Stockholmia förlag.

Lane, C. 2003. 'Stepping Out from Behind the Grand Silhouette – Joan Harrison's Films of the 1940s', in D.A. Gerstner and J. Geigner (eds), *Authorship and Film*. New York, Routledge, pp. 97–115.

Larsson, M. and A. Marklund (eds). 2010. *Swedish Film – An Introduction and Reader*. Lund: Nordic Academic Press.

Larz. 1940. Review of *With You in My Arms*, *Stockholms Tidningen*, 11 October, no page. Hasse Ekman Archives.

_____. 1942. Review of *Flames in the Dark*, *Stockholms Tidningen*, 3 March, no page. Hasse Ekman Archives.

Lindsay, V. 2000. *The Art of the Moving Picture*. New York: Modern Library.

Livingston, P. 2009. *Cinema, Philosophy, Bergman*. Oxford: Oxford University Press.

Löfgren, O. 2009. 'Turism och resande', in J. Christensson (ed.), *Signums svenska kulturhistoria 1900-tal*. Lund: Signum, pp. 199–233.

Magnusson, L. 2002. *Sveriges ekonomiska historia*, 3rd ed. Stockholm: Prisma.

Malgefors, L. 1961. 'Anti-Bergman-film i TV', *Röster i Radio/TV* 45, p. 26. Microfilm, Swedish Film Institute.

Mazierska, E. and L. Rascaroli. 2004. *The Cinema of Nanni Moretti: Dreams and Diaries*. London: Wallflower.

McCreary, E. 1976. 'Louis Delluc, Film Theorist, Critic and Prophet', *Cinema Journal* 16, 1, pp. 14–35.

McIlroy, B. 1986. *World Cinema 2: Sweden*. London: Flicks Books.

Naremore, J. 2014. *An Invention without a Future – Essays on Cinema*. Berkeley and Los Angeles: University of California Press.

Natzén, C. 2010. *The Coming of Sound Film in Sweden 1928–1932: New and Old Technologies*. Stockholm: Stockholm University.

Nowell-Smith, G. 2003. *Luchino Visconti*, 3rd ed. London: BFI.

Olsson, J. 1979. *Svensk film under andra världskriget*. Stockholm: Liber.

O'Regan, T. 1996. *Australian National Cinema*. London: Routledge.

OR.-t. 1941. Review of *The First Division*, *Dagens Nyheter*, 24 September, no page. Hasse Ekman Archives.

Partnoy, F. 2009. *The Match King: Ivar Kreuger and the Financial Scandal of the Century*. London: Profile Books.

Pavane. 1945. Review of *Wandering with the Moon*, *Bonniers Litterära Magasin (BLM)* 7, no page. Hasse Ekman Archives.

Perkins, V.F. 1993. *Film as Film: Understanding and Judging Movies.* New York: Da Capo Press.

Poague, L.A. 1978. *The Cinema of Ernst Lubitsch.* London: The Tantivy Press.

Powell, D. 1991. *The Dilys Powell Film Reader,* ed. C. Cook. Manchester: Carcanet.

Qvist, P.O. 1986. *Jorden är vår arvedel – landsbygden i svensk spelfilm 1940–1959.* Uppsala: Filmhäftet.

_____. 1995. *Folkhemmets bilder.* Lund: Studentlitteratur.

Ray, S. 1994. *Our Films, Their Films.* New York: Hyperion Books.

Ronci, M. 2008. 'De som inte fick plats – att hålla måttet', in J. af Geierstam (ed.), *Industrilandet.* Stockholm: Premiss, pp. 101–120.

Roth, H.I. 2004. 'Multi-cultural Sweden', in K. Almqvist and K. Glans (eds), *The Swedish Success Story?* trans. P. Fischer. Stockholm: Axel and Margaret Ax:son Johnson Foundation, pp. 213–226.

Rugg, L.H. 2005. 'Ingmar Bergman Projected', in A. Nestingen and T.G. Elkington (eds), *Transnational Cinema in a Global North.* Detroit: Wayne State University Press, pp. 221–241.

Sarris, A. 1968. *The American Cinema – Directors and Directions.* New York: E.P. Dutton & Co. Inc.

Schein, H. 1951. 'Fru Filmia som våldtagen', *BLM* 9, no page. Hasse Ekman Archives.

Schildt, J. 1970. *Det pensionerade paradiset – anteckningar om svensk 30-tals film.* Stockholm: PAN/Norstedts.

Snickars, P. 2008. 'Det medialiserande samhället', in J. af Geijerstam (ed.), *Industrilandet.* Stockholm: Premiss, pp. 171–201.

Södergran, E. 1980. *The Collected Poems of Edith Södergran.* Mullsjö, Anglo-American Center.

Soila, T. 1998. 'Sweden', in T. Soila, A. Söderbergh Widding and G. Iversen, *Nordic National Cinema.* London: Routledge, pp. 142–232.

Soila, T. (ed.). 2005. *The Cinema of Scandinavia.* London: Wallflower Press.

Soila, T., A. Söderbergh Widding and G. Iversen. 1998. *Nordic National Cinema.* London: Routledge.

Staiger, J. 2008. 'Analysing Self-Fashioning in Authoring and Reception', in M. Koskinen (ed.), *Ingmar Bergman: Revisited.* London: Wallflower, pp. 89–106.

Stam, R. 2000. *Film Theory: An Introduction.* Malden: Blackwell Publishing.

Svensson, G. 1941. *BLM* 6, pp. 483–484.

Tannefors, G. 1949. 'Hasse Ekman försök till porträtt av en artist', *Biografbladet* 3, pp. 176–184. Hasse Ekman Archive.

Udden, J. 2009. *No Man an Island: The Cinema of Hou Hsiao-Hsien.* Hong Kong: Hong Kong University Press.

Werner, G. 1978. *Den svenska filmens historia.* Stockholm: Norstedts.

Wernlöf. 1949. 'Publiken ska slippa se mig i nästa film säger Hasse E.', *Expressen,* 23 October, no page. Microfilm, Swedish Film Institute.

Widerberg, B. 1962. *Visionen i svensk film.* Stockholm: Bonniers.

Young, V. 1971. *Cinema Borealis: Ingmar Bergman and the Swedish Ethos.* New York: David Lewis.

Zack. 1950. Review of *The Kiss on the Cruise, Svenska Dagbladet,* 17 December, no page. Hasse Ekman Archives.

Zern, L. 1985. 'En svensk Truffaut', *Expressen,* 14 July. Microfilm, Swedish Film Institute.

The Hasse Ekman Archives are located at the Swedish Film Institute in Stockholm, Sweden.

Index